Making Friends

Making Friends

···················· A GUIDE TO ····················
Understanding and Nurturing
YOUR CHILD'S FRIENDSHIPS
···

ELIZABETH HARTLEY-BREWER

Da Capo
∞
LIFE
LONG

A Member of the Perseus Books Group

This North American edition of *Making Friends* by Elizabeth Hartley-Brewer, first published in the United Kingdom in 2009 as *Making Sense of Your Child's Friendships*, is published by arrangement with Piccadilly Press Limited, London, England.

Designed by Trish Wilkinson
Set in 12-point Goudy by the Perseus Books Group

Library of Congress Cataloging-in-Publication Data

Hartley-Brewer, Elizabeth.
    Making friends : a guide to understanding and nurturing your child's friendships / Elizabeth Hartley-Brewer.
        p.   cm.
    ISBN 978-0-7382-1323-1 (alk. paper)
    1. Friendship in children. 2. Interpersonal relations in children. I. Title.
BF723.F68H37 2009
155.4'18—dc22   2009005721

First Da Capo Press edition 2009

Published by Da Capo Press
A Member of the Perseus Books Group
www.dacapopress.com

Da Capo Press books are available at special discounts for bulk purchases in the U.S. by corporations, institutions, and other organizations. For more information, please contact the Special Markets Department at the Perseus Books Group, 2300 Chestnut Street, Suite 200, Philadelphia, PA, 19103, or call (800) 810-4145, ext. 5000, or e-mail special.markets@perseusbooks.com.

10 9 8 7 6 5 4 3 2 1

For KB and Angela,
friends since childhood,
and Richard

CONTENTS

INTRODUCTION

Research for this book produced several surprises for me. I had seen from my own experiences as an active mom and stepmom for more than three decades that friends are desperately important to most children, most of the time. Having written previously about eight- to twelve-year-olds, the "tween" age group, I felt I understood a great deal about the ups and downs of children's close and not-so-close relationships at an age when children become noticeably hungry for friends. I remember those roller-coaster friendship years so well!

What I didn't fully realize before I interviewed and chatted with children across the age range, and with many parents, in order to find out more about how children view their friendships, was that what children want, or get, from their friends and how important friendships are to them change in specific and important ways throughout childhood—well before the tween years. I realized that even one-year-olds can show delight when they're with particular children they see frequently: For younger children, smiles and laughter are key signals of friendship. But I also learned how some older children seek friends as much to protect themselves against being bullied or picked on as to have fun and feel accepted within their social group.

When my eleven-year-old stepson and nine-year-old stepdaughter came to live with me and their dad, having spent two years in the United States with their mom and stepdad, the friends they made at their new school were central to helping them adjust and settle into an unfamiliar place. Joining them later, my own two children—also a boy and a girl— had very different patterns of friendship from each other and from the older two. Not having access to either cell phones or social networking sites until well into their teens, their lives were less complicated than those of today's children, whose exposure to text messaging and computers has big downsides as well as major upsides. The possibility of cyber bullying, for example, was not something I had to contemplate until my daughter was at least fifteen. I hear so much from anxious parents about the amount of bullying that takes place in school and now can continue after school online. I was aware with my daughter that the pressure to have ever more glamorous birthday parties to go one better than her friends (or other moms) was growing; but in the past ten years both the options for entertainment and the money to pay for it have grown and the pressure has intensified. On top of this, the marketing industry targets brands at ever younger kids, making the competition between children to own particular items far tougher for parents to handle.

I'm also aware that researchers and psychologists who work with children are only now appreciating how much friends influence even younger children's development. It seemed a good moment, then, not only to talk to children and parents in greater depth about friendships but also to record these conversations to help parents understand and better manage a central part of their child's life.

This book is the result. It focuses on children's typical friendship experiences in pre-adolescence, particularly during their elementary school years, and explains why friendships develop in the way they do. It also looks at how your role as a parent needs to adapt in response, from directing and fixing your children's friendships at the beginning to staying in the background once they are settled in middle school. Many of the interviews conducted for this book were with British children, but my interviews with American children assured me that children's experiences of friendship and the issues surrounding it are universal.

Most advice for parents tends to focus on adolescent friendships, no doubt because more is at stake when they go wrong. But as we now know and appreciate that children's earlier friendships have a powerful influence on their developing identity and longer-term social and emotional health, happiness, and well-being, it's important to understand younger children's experiences, too. Teenagers who have problems making and keeping friends, or who get in with or seem attracted to the wrong crowd, have often had similar difficulties and styles of relationships in the years preceding adolescence, which means that the sooner you spot an emerging problem and respond to it appropriately, the better.

If you wait until your child's teenage years before you take action, it becomes much harder to intervene. During early and mid-childhood, however, it is part of our parental duty to encourage, preserve, and monitor friendships: This can be a very intensive process, as the issues and dilemmas appear, if not daily, then (typically) weekly, for girls especially. Such involvement can make us feel our child's pain and anguish intensely when things are difficult for her and we feel responsible.

Of course, children's elementary school friendships are generally transient. Though some do stand the test of time, most will not survive into adolescence, and even fewer remain into adulthood. There are good developmental reasons for this, as we shall see. Early friendships can also fizzle out or get eclipsed when children change schools, move, or follow very different paths post-school. Yet *transient* does not mean insignificant or unimportant, which would be a typical "grown-up" mistake to make. To each child at that point in his or her life, any particular friend can mean the world, and it's important for us to remember this. We need to see the experience from the child's perspective, to have and retain a sense of proportion as we provide the shoulder to cry on or act as the metaphorical cushion to punch as he or she relieves frustration or even grief at the latest insult from, or apparent loss of, a special friend.

The key difference between children's friendships and those of adults is that whereas adults on the whole choose to be friends with people who have shared similar experiences or share similar interests or characteristics (people whom they know they can trust and whose company they still find enjoyable), children are still growing and finding out about themselves. They're learning about who they are and whom they get along with best; discovering different ways to manage conflict and to compromise and share. They're also finding out just how far they can go in being direct and open and discovering when it might be better to be quiet and exercise discretion. As adults, we would seriously consider dropping someone who started to be overly critical or extremely thoughtless and selfish. Children, though, both are more needy of friends and have fewer expectations of appropriate behavior from someone who claims to be a friend. Younger children are also far less judgmental. They haven't yet developed the cognitive skills to judge in a critical manner and will often tolerate behavior we would find unacceptable. And, of course, as children, they understand all too well the temperamental and emotional outbursts of other children and will tend to see them in context.

Children learn a great many useful life lessons from friendship problems. It is, almost always, a mistake to step in too soon to protect them from this—sometimes literally—hands-on learning. It is also a mistake to assume that every child, either boy or girl, is going to have the same pattern of friends as you do. Children are different from each other and different from their parents. Some prefer to have, or simply end up with, a larger group of friends with no one person standing out as a special friend. Some will be content with serial best friends, just one or two of them at a time, and are not, therefore, invited to all the parties but are content. And some children are quite happy with few, or no, particular friends. These children will often have passions and interests that they can follow intently at home and may find the general play of the playground dull. As parents, we need to remember to accept a range of friendship patterns in our children's lives, and if a child surprises or disappoints us, not imply to him that he is inadequate in any way.

The greatest dilemma any parent faces is whether, and how far, to get involved either in a child's making friends or in sorting out disagreements between friends. It's hard to resist when our child seems intensely distressed. How to balance our response is addressed throughout this book: My hope is that parents will be able to refer to this book when different issues arise at different ages in a child's life and that parents will gain some insight and understanding as well as a range of useful responses. No one should try to dictate what to do in any particular situation, as there are frequently subtleties that might suggest one action rather than another more obvious one; nevertheless, certain responses from us generally are helpful while others seem to make things worse. By recounting real children's and parents' stories, I hope parents will get a sense for which strategies and responses are likely to work best for them.

1

THE FOUR PHASES OF FRIENDSHIP

How Friendship Grows and Changes Before and Through Elementary School

There is far more to our children's friendships than meets the eye. Children change and mature dramatically, which inevitably affects their friendships; however, the changes occur so gradually that they often go unnoticed by us, the parents and caregivers. They happen in response to children's natural cognitive and emotional development—their capacity to think about, relate to, and understand their world and the people in it—rather than to any practical aspect of home or school. In order to be supportive when things go wrong, it is useful for us to understand the typical phases of friendship that preteen children experience.

The Four Phases of Friendship

Phase One: Pre-friendship—Making Sociable Moments Comfortable (One Month to Four Years Old)

Although very young children do not make friends in a meaningful sense, even babies and young children who see others regularly do seem to pick out and enjoy the company of particular children, or be indifferent to or even apparently irritated by others. Smiles, squeals, wriggles, and jiggles are all signs that a young toddler is pleased to see a "friend." Parents and caregivers who meet regularly with a small group of friends with similar-aged children provide a springboard for early friendships. I once attended a multiple first birthday party organized by several moms who'd become friends at a local childbirth class during pregnancy. Their babies knew each other quite well by then, and I was struck by one little boy, Daniel, who was obviously fixated by the shiny dark hair of the only girl who had flowing locks—the others were still almost bald. Whenever she came near him, he scrambled (he wasn't yet walking) to get closer to stroke her and her hair! He clearly loved to be near her and loved her softness. Daniel and another girl there, Katie, were close in another way because they'd been looked after by the same nanny for almost a year. Now, nine months later, when they see each other, they wriggle their arms about, smile broadly, run toward each other, and hold hands, showing great pleasure and excitement. By contrast, Katie tends to turn away and ignore Grace, a serious little girl who doesn't smile much, when she comes over with her mom.

Even at this young age, and despite their inability to talk to each other, children can benefit socially and emotionally from having regular time with familiar babies and the familiar adults accompanying them, especially if there is a routine surrounding those particular times together. Young children soon recognize the faces of those they see regularly and associate particular sounds and games with particular people. These encounters, at home, in the park or local café, or at playgroup, help young children to view other children as part of their widening social world and as a source of pleasure. Of course, once children reach age three, most will go to preschool and spend regular time with others without a parent in tow. A kindergarten class teacher told me she can tell when a new pupil has attended preschool because he finds it easier to play and make friends. This does not mean that a child who has spent most of her time at home before starting formal school will be set back for very long, but it may take more time for that child to open herself up and make a friend because she'll have to negotiate those initial steps first.

Phase Two: The Kindergarten and First Grade Years (Five to Seven Years Old)

When children start kindergarten, their friendships tend to be founded on coincidence and convenience, and they are famously fickle. It's the "easy come, easy go" phase. Friends come and go with a speed and ease that make some parents worry about their child's ability to make meaningful friends. What it shows, though, is that children of this age invest a lot less of themselves in their individual friendships than older children and adults do. Friendship at this stage depends overwhelmingly on accessibility: the person they sit

TIPS . . . to help your preschooler settle in comfortably

- Children feel safe with routines, so changes to their schedule may cause distress—on top of coping with the new setting. Introduce some features of the new routine a few days before your child starts so it feels familiar. Keep it as simple and relaxed as possible, with time for him to adjust himself.
- Let him take in something from home that he can show either to his teacher or to another child, to help him make that first contact and feel part of the group.
- Taking in a flower, pretty leaf, or smooth, shiny stone for his teacher will help him to feel connected and friendly toward him or her.
- If he's crying at the door before you leave or when he arrives, give him a couple of minutes to try to compose himself.
- Tell him what you'll be doing while he's gone and mention a treat for his homecoming.
- If you have a pet at home that he's fond of, draw a picture of it or take a photograph and place it in a pocket, so he feels accompanied by a furry friend at least.
- If you need to leave home *now* and he's still resisting, pick him up rather than drag him by his arm. Suggest he may fear that he won't cope but you know he'll manage really well.
- Ask him to find out the names of two other children there so he can tell these to you when you see him later.

next to in the classroom; the one who goes to the same swimming class; the boy who lives next door or on the floor below; and, still very important, your good friend's son or daughter if they are of similar age. The friendships that are given the space to take root and flourish are almost always parent-led—"Wouldn't you like to have Sara over to play? She seems like a nice girl!" "Katy and Martha are coming over for coffee tomorrow morning, so you'll be able to spend time playing with Jo and Darrel. That'll be fun for you!"

Imaginary Friends

Your child's imagination helps to make him the unique individual that he is. Imagination fuels curiosity and creates energy, which children need to help them grow and develop. Imagination also makes children impulsive and immediate. They want things now. So when there is no one else around to be a real-life playmate, an imaginary friend is likely to appear to fill the gap. These companions—and this is the best bit—can be conjured up at will. If your child has a rich fantasy life with imaginary friends, it should be seen as evidence of having a healthy mind, not an embarrassing quirk. Imaginary friends will be covered in more detail in the next chapter.

Waiting for Real Friends to Appear

When children first start school, finding friends and then having the confidence to ask them over is a sign of being happy, settled, and liked. Parents are usually desperate for that moment to arrive, partly so that they can relax knowing that their child is normal and perhaps partly so they can get some time off through arranged play dates! It can be tempting to invite someone over or to push your child to accept an invitation before he's ready. But a child who has just started at "big school" needs a while to adjust—there are new rules, larger and much noisier groups, and they need to wait longer to get and receive less individual attention. It is exhausting to talk to and deal with a large number of unfamiliar children. It's hard even for us when we go somewhere where we know only a few people, or when we have to make conversation with a stranger for any length of time. For most young children, this forced socializing and acclimatization is sufficiently demanding to tire them out totally for weeks.

Adjusting to Big School

During this difficult time when children are coping with so many new things, they need the familiarity and stability of house and home and the warmth of your love and approval far more than they need friends. Kindergarten teachers generally advise that children should not have after-school arrangements set up for them until they ask, and most children won't be ready for a few months into the school year. Even if your child has attended a nursery or playgroup five days a week and played with other children regularly, school is a dramatic change and they will need you more.

Katy, mother of five-year-old Madeline, said, "She attended full-time pre-school before she started big school, so I thought it would be a breeze. She was used to long days out. But I couldn't get over how totally exhausted she was. It was the bigger groups, the bigger children and the noise, and not being able to do what she wanted. She point-blank refused to have any child back home for six months. It's only now, though, since the spring, that she's happy for this to happen. She didn't mind going to someone else's home, but hers was absolutely out of bounds to others."

There are other reasons, apart from sheer tiredness, why young boys and girls aren't raring to go in the race to build an impressive social life. Young children sometimes find it hard to integrate home and school or simply prefer to keep home separate. It is *their* place, and they don't want to share it or you—like a favorite teddy or toy. If you have ever been into your child's classroom to help with an activity, you may have been shocked to realize how possessive your child is, to hear her exclaim in puzzled and hurt tones, "She's *my* mommy—I should have her first!" or "No, it's my turn again!" She can hardly bear to have any other child get close or have your attention, and can assert her special claim only by having a second slot of time and attention at the end of your allotted session as well. This certainly happened to me when I went to both of my children's schools. This sense of ownership is also shown by the forlorn, even desperate, look on their faces when they emerge from school, keen to be scooped up, repossessed, and taken home by their parent or caregiver only to find this person absorbed in conversation with another parent.

If your child has not yet asked to have a friend over after school, it doesn't necessarily mean that he's not making good friends during the day. He'd just prefer them to stay in that realm and not enter his other world. He may well have favorite people to paint with, others that he may choose as a dressing up partner, or someone to do puzzles with or run around with at recess—yet he may not be ready to have them come home and share his mom or his private space.

TIPS . . . for the first weeks and months of kindergarten

- Realize they need to be with you at home.
- Don't force friends on your child—wait for him to ask to have someone over.
- Accept that he'll make friends more easily if he feels secure with you and knows that there's no pressure.
- Appreciate that he'll be making friends in class but may not want to play with them anywhere else. You can explain this to the parent/caregiver if he's invited to another child's house and doesn't want to go.

Chopping and Changing

Five- to seven-year-olds, especially girls, can seem to have a different friend every week. Rupert, age nine, said of his seven-year-old sister, "She comes home with a new best friend every day!" This can occur because they have been paired with a different child than usual to do some class-work or they happen to have found someone new to play with at recess. Younger children are very egocentric and im-mediate and don't yet have sophisticated thoughts. The person they have just had a nice time with, whom they have just decided they like, is now their latest friend, who temporarily eclipses all others.

Loyalty is a sophisticated notion that takes time to grasp, and it is only when children grow older that it becomes a feature of friendship. Although the latest friend looms large to the point that another child may be pushed from their thoughts, one new friend does not, in fact, mean that another has to be dropped and treated as a nonfriend to make room: The superseded one may merely have been put out of mind for a while—that is, a case of "out of sight, out of mind." After the next close encounter, that individual will probably reappear as their special friend. This is quite normal. Six-year-old Annie Rose put it well: "Say, every day you make a new friend and then you break up with them and then the next playtime you're back friends again!" Though you may be tempted to tease your child about the jack-in-a-box, on-off style of relationship, it's best to say nothing, smile to yourself quietly, and let it pass without comment.

Changing Their Minds About Going Over to Play

Mom was putting on Jessie's coat to go in the car to play at Casey's house when Jessie suddenly became tearful. "I don't want to go to Casey's house anymore. Mom, I don't want to go. I want to stay here with you." "Well, you've got to go. Why didn't you tell me this earlier today? I've got something I've fixed and it's too late now to pull out. Sorry, but that's it. Now, get out the door and into the car. What's the problem?" "I just don't want to go. Don't feel like it. I want to be here. Why do I have to go if I don't want to? Mom, let me stay here!" And with that, Jessie sat down on the floor in the doorway.

A common feature of friendships during this phase is children's tendency to get cold feet at the last minute, just as they're about to leave home to go over to another child's home to play or for a party—especially if this is an occasion when you were planning to leave them there and not socialize with the other parent at the same time.

There may be tears or tantrums if you insist that they go. Of course, this can be hugely inconvenient and embarrassing. It's natural to worry that your child's refusal will be seen as a rejection and insult that could end the friendship—and upset the parent, whom you may like and want as a friend, too. Yet a young child's sudden refusal is more likely to reflect his own uncertainty and insecurity than any worry about the other playmate's temperament, parent, or home circumstance. He may be anxious about what could happen at home while he's away from it, as well as worried about getting homesick and possibly creating a scene.

Only you can decide what's right for your child, as you know him best. No significant long-term harm will be done in selecting either approach suggested below, provided you don't make a habit of pushing him to go against his will when you have no other commitment to justify doing so.

Phase Three: The Middle Childhood Years (Seven to Ten Years Old)

The most noticeable change in the lives of seven- to ten-year-olds is their growing focus on friends. Around the age of seven or eight, most children become achingly hungry

TIPS . . . on what to try if your child's a habitual visit refuser

Encourage your child to go, to prove that he can cope with this situation, which should then boost his confidence.

- Offer to stay for a short while, which could make him feel easier about going.
- Arrange with the other mom just beforehand that he go for less time.
- Offer a small incentive if he stays the whole time. Alternatively, you might prefer to let him follow his instincts and show that you understand and trust him.
- Phone and cancel on this occasion.
- For the next play date, ask him if he'd like to go. If he agrees yet when the time comes changes his mind, it's a move forward. Still, don't force it.
- If the refusals continue, offer to stay for a while and tell him you will pick him up a bit early, to let him see he can manage.
- Praise him for whatever he's able to manage; say you expect he's pleased that it went well, and comment that you were confident he'd be fine.

for friends. As friends become more important, family becomes slowly but progressively less so. The changes that take place in children's brains as a normal part of growing up—psychologists call it *cognitive development*—enable children to think in more abstract ways. Middle childhood, as this period is referred to, is the time when children begin to see themselves as separate beings and move apart from their families emotionally; they remain reliant on their family

but no longer wholly dependent on it for identity, entertainment, and affirmation. They begin to "find their own
feet" and to seek friends to widen their horizon, to confirm
that they are likeable and that they can survive in the wider
world that they now know exists beyond their home.

Choosing Their Own Friends

The key words that characterize this phase of friendship are
choice, *autonomy*, *independence*, *influence*, *exploration*, and
fun. Children are no longer content to have the friends that
parents sift and select for them, or to spend time with children whom they chanced to meet or sit with; they now want
to choose their own friends, against very clear criteria. And
they have to if they are to fulfill their new requirement to
have friends who are like them, with whom they click; who
are interested in similar things, have a similar sense of humor, and with whom they can explore new opportunities,
learn new things, and become more independent and have
fun. This is the age and stage during which children experiment, explore, and confirm who they think they are by
choosing friends they think—perhaps subconsciously—are
like them. They say, in effect, "This is me; this is what I have
to offer. I think I am like you in this or that way; do you
agree, and do you like me?" If the person accepts the friendship, the implication is, "Hey, yes, I like you and I agree I'm
a lot like you." When this happens, the child can feel not
only accepted and likeable but also confident in her sense of

self and how she reads other people. It will help to boost her self-esteem, to be more outgoing, and to keep her confidence afloat.

> Paul, who was nearly nine, came home from his first day back at school extremely excited. "There's a new boy in my class," he explained, "and he's just like me! He plays the trumpet . . . loves nature, is interested in tanks and planes and . . . fishing!" Paul and the new boy soon bonded. Their friendship enabled them to carve out developmentally important private space— time alone together away from their parents in which they could explore their common interests and develop themselves, have fun, and become independent. The two boys became inseparable and are still best friends twenty years later.

Trust and Loyalty

Of course, making friends is not always straightforward and easy. Children who are still learning the ropes of relationships can misjudge them and are bound to make mistakes. They'll almost certainly go through a number of friends until they find one who's the best fit *and* trustworthy, and even then they can be let down and can be unsure how enduring a friendship is after time apart. By the end of phase three, children begin to see friends as more than someone they like and click with—they also expect a friend to be loyal, trusting, and to offer intimacy—someone to whom they can tell secrets and discuss personal matters with. Initially, that requires regular time together to build up trust and check out loyalty. When children don't see school friends during the long summer, it can create uncertainty. Lucy, age nine, said as the start of the new school year loomed, "It's funny, not being sure who your friends are until school starts again." She was concerned in case the closeness she felt she had with certain friends was misjudged.

TIPS . . . to get the friendship ball rolling when school restarts

- Suggest that she invite a friend over to play before school begins, to start the friendship ball rolling again.
- Realize that she's likely to be more tired than usual during those first stressful weeks.
- Make sure she has opportunities to talk to you.
- Realize that her concerns about the coming year may be reflected in more challenging behavior and try to be patient.
- Spend some fun time together so she knows she has your love and support whatever may happen at school.

Getting back into the routine of school can be emotionally exhausting and makes learning more difficult. Psychologists know that every year in September children's reading standards drop for about a month, along with other cognitive skills. The effort needed to get back into the habit of learning can mean that their social skills take a battering, too. It is not at all surprising that children can seem permanently exhausted and bad tempered in the first week or two, and this is more marked at the start of a school year.

Same-Gender Friendships

The one feature almost all seven- to ten-year-olds display is having same-gender friendships. Until this time, children can be happy to play a wide range of games with either boys or girls, often in mixed groups. Up to the age of about six, birthday parties are often mixed affairs and even best friends can be the opposite gender. This third phase, however, marks the complete parting of the ways. It marks, in fact, the developmental moment when gender takes center stage in children's identity. They now need to explore what being a boy or a girl means and how they might need to adjust their previous behavior and relationships accordingly.

Pulling Rank: How Behavior Can Border on the Bullying

The journey through these three or four years of middle childhood can be tough. Children this age are trying to make their mark, so there can be a constant undercurrent of competition as they pitch themselves and pull rank in the attempt to be top dog. Gossip mongering and spreading rumors are common tactics for children of this age, especially for less secure youngsters who are trying to cope with self-doubt. They often target those with oodles of coveted confidence.

These seven- to ten-year-olds can also enjoy teasing and may try to get their own way through manipulating others. The jostling for position can border on bullying. The most common and potentially destructive form of bullying among this age group is what can be dubbed "relationship bullying"—tactics such as name-calling and cold-shouldering someone. As having a friend starts to *really* matter during this phase, this is the time when relationship bullies develop vampire-like, full-length fangs to exert maximum damage. Those who feel the need to hurt and parade their power target others in the place where it will hurt most—someone's ability to make and keep friends and even his capacity to be a good or fun friend.

Phase Four: The Transition Years—Win Some, Lose Some (Ten to Twelve Years Old)

"The one thing you want is friends," Alice said, as she described her tense and difficult experiences negotiating the shark-filled waters that can surround the move to middle school or junior high. She had felt cut off and cut out, as all her previous friends were going elsewhere. It can be a nerve-wracking time; and when this new phase of friendship-making goes wrong, it can sour a child's attitude toward middle school and put her off learning for a long time.

Worry About Losing Friends

By the age of eleven, friends are central to your child's sense of self and self-esteem. In the lead-up to switching schools, it's entirely normal for your eleven-year-old to fret over whether anyone will like her at her new school, worry about any informal style rules she may infringe unknowingly, and be unsure which of her interests or which aspect of her personality to draw attention to as she presents herself in a new environment. Anyone who is undergoing such a big change will lose some confidence in her sense of self and become confused about who she really is, making the fight for friends even more frantic.

Thirteen-year-old Alice remembered what it was like for her: "I wanted to find a best friend as soon as possible. I knew that the longer I left it, the more likely there'd be no one left for me. So I jumped in and, as time proved, jumped too soon because my choice was very bad. Sally was a nightmare and caused me such grief. But you have to go through that to learn. Parents can't do this for you."

Still, other children feel both anxiety and excitement about moving on. Emma, age eleven, told me, "I'm lucky because I'm going to a school where most of my friends are going. But I don't think this will make much difference because our group is falling apart. . . . It's hard. I think we'll all be making new friends when we get there. But sometimes in my group we talk about middle school already. It's really good. We talk about worries and friends. . . . I'm not as scared about going as I thought I'd be. My only fear is not to make any friends and have all my friends leaving me."

Mark, age eleven, explained that "to make a friend at the new school I'll go next to someone who's sad. I'll say, 'Are you okay? Can I be your friend?'" Selin, also age eleven, said, "I'm worried about losing my friends. But if I don't make new friends I'll still have my old ones. I'd look for honesty in a new friend." Leanne, also eleven, and Selin's best friend, said, "Even though Selin's my friend and we're going to the same school, getting to know someone new you're going to have to leave them anyway. But I'll still see her." Jodie, a classmate, was quite upbeat. "It'll be easy to find a new friend. I'll look for someone who'll help me with my work and play with me."

Eleven-year-old Katherine said, "I feel good about it. I'll make new friends and also keep my old friends. I can meet a lot of new people by talking. I'm definitely going to keep friends with Sarah. I definitely want to branch out. I'm interested in going to middle school to see how much work there is. I really hope that all the teachers are nice." Other children were concerned about making friends too quickly before they really knew them. One boy said, "We've had years to get to know people here."

Friends, Identity, and Self-esteem

"I couldn't be without friends," said Selin, who was discussing the prospect of losing her good friends upon changing schools. "They're like a part of my life. Without friends I'd feel like nothing. Nothing." Katherine described what she looked for in a good friend: "A good friend is a person that's nice and doesn't do mean jokes. She likes hanging around with you, and it doesn't matter what you wear. A person who really relates to you and likes what you're doing. Like my friend Sarah. We talk 12–7. . . . We compliment each other all the time because we think we're the coolest divas. That's basically what I look for. They like you just for who you are." These two comments show vividly the role friends play for most children at this age in framing their identity and maintaining their self-esteem. It's not surprising that worry about losing friends and being without any, along with fear of being bullied, is such a common concern among eleven-year-olds who are facing middle school. Here are some concerns children have raised with me:

> "We're used to being the cats and now we'll have to be the mice."
> "I'm not ready for it. I want to stay here one more year. I like it here."
> "It feels like we're having to jump off a cliff."
> "I'm worried about not being liked and being late and getting a detention. I'm sad to leave, especially [since] one of my friends isn't coming to my new school."

Arming Themselves in Advance

The horror of being without a friend in the new school leads many children to adjust their friendships ahead of time, perhaps to arm themselves against the potential humiliation of being seen without friends and therefore being unlovable and also to protect them from possible bullying.

Once children know which new school is to be theirs, they often begin to seek out others going to the same school and drop their former bosom pals. It can be painful for children who are suddenly sidelined or otherwise replaced. The experience can be especially brutal when there is competition for places at particular private schools and when towns accord higher status to certain schools over others. Having friends going to the same school, however snatched and shallow and temporary the friendships may be, provides comfort during this otherwise difficult transition.

Thea was having a hard time in her elementary school. She was being bullied, largely, she felt, because she was the only white girl in her class and only one of three in the school, which was in a very racially mixed area. She had found some comfort in a new friendship with Maya, a lonely girl in the grade above who lived close to her home, and each was the other's lifeline as they could play together out of school, too. But halfway through Maya's last year, she suddenly dumped Thea. She was now keen to get close to the girls in her class who were moving to the same middle school. Even outside school, at the end of the day, and on holidays and weekends, Maya ignored Thea. Despite their previous shared vulnerability and closeness, she had no thought for the upset that she was causing her abandoned "best" friend.

Cyber Friends

In the final year or two of elementary school, children often have the computer and cognitive skills to make friends in

▦ TIPS . . . for giving support over friendship worries

If your child feels abandoned . . .

- Explain that her friend is seeking out people going to the same school, and why.
- Show that you understand how unpleasant this can feel.
- Reassure her by suggesting she invite over another child who's still friendly.
- If you had a similar experience at any time, tell her about it.
- Point out that any advantage from having friends in tow is only temporary as most children will forge new friendships after a short while.

If your child is going to a different school from most of his friends . . .

- Help him to feel confident. Although it's natural to worry about being left with no one, assure him that his personality and kind nature will guarantee him friends.
- Let him know that he can continue to see old friends on weekends.
- Reassure him that everyone else will be feeling exactly the same.
- Suggest he could attend an after-school club that matches an interest of his to meet someone with similar interests.
- Explain that friendships based on similar interests and outlook take time to find and it's worth waiting a while to get it right rather than rushing in.
- Ask the new school if there is any way for new pupils to meet each other before starting school. Perhaps it issues a class address list or there's a school website or social networking site so your child can be introduced to others joining his class from different schools and establish a cyber friendship before the real thing can start.

cyberspace. These are "virtual" friends whom your child may never meet yet nonetheless feel close to. This new world brings the possibility of pretending to be different people with different correspondents; and, of course, exposure to cyber bullying and predatory pedophiles. Virtual friends are not quite the same as the fantasy-inspired imaginary friends of early childhood: Virtual friends certainly entail the use of imagination but, unlike imaginary friends, are real people (unless this is abused).

● ● ●

Watching your child begin to enjoy the company of other children, form particular friendships, and then grow in confidence through having fun and going out with them as he grows older is one of the delights of being a parent. Each phase brings its particular rewards but also, of course, its own challenges and concerns for both you and your child—worries about fitting in, being accepted, getting in with the "right" or "wrong" crowd, and the gossip and manipulation that increasingly pervades life in school. We look at these potential problems later. First, we consider the different types of friends a child may have, and why, to help you make greater sense of your child's particular choices.

2

WHAT, AND WHO,
IS A "FRIEND"?

Philosophers have tried for centuries to define what friendship actually is. Some friends fall into our life. Others we spot as interesting and gently make a play for them. Many adult friendships are forged through their children having become friends or the coincidence of being neighbors. Making friends seems easier at certain periods in life than at others, and friendships can fade or change over time. Friendship serves up both pleasure and disappointment. It is no surprise, then, that elementary-school-aged children can and do get confused when someone whom they thought was a friend turns out not to be so kind and straightforward; and that when they complain to us about a friend's bad treatment they don't necessarily want to be told to stop being that person's friend. This chapter sets out to try to explain how children's views of their friendships change over time and then looks at different types of friends, ending with a short discussion of the difference between popularity and friendship.

Children's Developing Views of Friendship

Michael was in the last year at his elementary school when he was "taken for a ride" by his supposed friends. A group of boys in his class got together to create a spoof birthday party that was never going to take place. They prepared invitations, and of course Michael received one; they talked in advance about the party, to reinforce its reality; and on the afternoon before the party they left the school playground shouting "See you tomorrow!" to Michael. But when he turned up at the nominated house at the declared time with his mom, who had driven him, there was no one there and nothing happening. He realized only then that it was a scam.

Michael's mother was furious. She insisted that none of the boys involved who had claimed to be her son's friend would be allowed into her house again. Indeed, she felt so humiliated that she decided he wasn't allowed to see them socially anywhere else, either. Michael, though, saw it differently. He claimed that these boys were still his friends, said he could handle the embarrassment, and told his mom to lay off. He was, in fact, far less affronted by his friends' behavior than by his mother's—as he saw it—overreaction and interference.

Was this scam a form of unacceptable bullying, as the mother thought, with her son as the victim and now in need of her protection? Was Michael so desperate for friends that he was prepared to shrug off the insult and try again? Did he, perhaps, feel that to avoid playing the victim he should simply pull himself together and appear unaffected—and certainly keep his mom well out of it? Or did Michael genuinely bear no grudge, believing that these boys were simply practicing and enjoying their skill at arranging pranks, a very typical pastime of boys that age, with no malice intended?

It turned out that Michael was closer to the truth than his mother. What this story shows is that parents don't always get it right: Friends can be playful, to the point of hurtful, and sometimes stretch loyalty to a point where the friendship can be questioned. Nothing about friendship in action is straightforward.

It is not easy to help our children think in simple terms about different types of friends or what they should expect from a friend. Young children are limited by their vocabulary: Children typically begin to use the word *friend* sometime after their third birthday. Children learn about intimacy, how to make and sustain relationships, and how to "read" and trust other people and learn about themselves as they argue, fight, get jealous, break up, and make up. This is a necessary part of childhood. Only when they accumulate a wide range of experience will they be able to attach meaning to the various words we use to describe different levels of friendship.

Preschool—Phase One

Up to the age of four or five, a child may describe or identify someone as a friend but will have little idea of what is really meant by that other than "This person makes me feel good and I like to have her around." When you watch children at work and play in preschool settings, it is evident that certain children are attracted to each other and enjoy being in the company of the other. Their first understanding of friendship is closely tied to "liking"—whatever they understand by that. At this age, of course, they—and we—will be using the word *like* to describe a range of preferences, including types of food: "I like ice cream best," for example. This point illustrates the limitations of a young child's vocabulary.

Kindergarten—Phase Two

The next stage of understanding occurs when children refer to liking someone because they are "kind." Hannah, age six, spoke of her friendship with Leyla: "We've been friends since preschool. Our mommies were friends, and we made friends too. We play mommies and sisters. We take turns at being each. I got lots of other friends—Lucy, Courtney, Morgan. I play with them. They're kind. Leyla likes my baby stroller." "Yes," Leyla confirmed, "she has the best toys! And she eats fries and fish fingers!" Joey said, "I like Luke because he's kind. He's been twelve times to my house, and I let him choose a game to play. I liked Luke and was trying to be his friend. I got Luke a tissue he needed and he thought I was kind." Luke said, "Joey and I are friends because when I was in kindergarten we was playing together and then became friends. When I fell, he went to Mrs. Findlay." Casey, age six, said, "Being a friend is being kind."

Kindness is judged by gestures, such as those described by the children noted in the previous paragraph, and by smiles.

When asked "How do you make friends?" Casey replied, "You're playing with them and they're smiling and you smile back." Smiles are an important part of making up after a disagreement, too. "After, we gave smiles to each other and we all shaked hands." A smile is a simple, direct, and immediate way to start an encounter that doesn't give too much away if it's not reciprocated. Having "kind" friends who respond in friendly ways clearly helps younger children to feel safe.

Middle Childhood—Phase Three

By the time children are seven or eight, their idea of what a friend is changes yet again. It becomes much more important to them to have an interest or experience in common with a friend. Children at this age are inclined to pair up with someone who is not just likeable but is also like them and like-minded, and this is as true for children who are obliging and "good" as it is for the mischievous ones. A child who already feels that he can do nothing right and is constantly described as "bad" is likely to make friends with other naughty children. Michelle and Sarah, both nine years old, are best friends. When asked why they were special to each other, Sarah said, "We're into the same things. . . . We've been friends for five years. And now we both wear glasses!" Joseph said of his best friend, "We both like the same football team and trading cards." His friend, Kailen, said, "I like computer stuff and . . . we also like to play hide-and-seek."

The Transition Year—Phase Four

When a chid is about ten years old, the notion of friendship
further develops to embrace more complex expectations such
as loyalty, trust and sharing (sharing involves trust, because
you expect to get it back), and sticking together through
thick and thin. However, being kind and caring remain important core qualities. In a group discussion on the imminent
move to middle school with ten- and eleven-year-olds and
the need, then, to find new friends, Seth said, "A friend would
go to a bully and say 'stop'; a friend will stick up for you—
when you're hurt or someone's making fun of you." He continued, "A friend is someone you can trust with secrets, who's
kind; 95 percent is whether I can trust a friend, someone you
can tell a secret to. They'll also treat you as special, give you
things." Ellie reflected a common belief that you can trust a
friend to return things such as rulers, pens, and personal items
that you lend to them, and introduced a new idea: listening.
She said, "A friend is when you borrow things together, their
personality is kindness and caring, and they listen to you."
During this phase, children become more acutely aware of being let down, of trust being abused. Joe said warily, "You have
to be careful of friends who turn out not to be friends. . . . I
lent my game to [someone] and he wiped all the data before
he gave it back to me. And I was nearly at the top level!"

Ten-year-olds are aware of, and able to express, the complex nature of relationships—and the need to be on their
guard. Friends can be tricky as well as affirming, and they
certainly are now more inclined to test their power on those

close to them. A child may set up a challenge specifically to test the true loyalty of a declared friend, or may use a friend's need for loyalty to threaten the friendship, to desta-bilize the individual and thereby keep the upper hand in the relationship. We'll return to this later, in Chapter 5.

Friendship As Armor: Protection and Defense

A common and very important theme emerged from my many conversations with youngsters from a wide age range: A friend is essentially someone with whom you feel safe; someone who will look after you, look out for you, whom you can lean on, and who will respect your privacy and vul-nerability. Although friends can be entertaining and fun, they also provide a considerable measure of protection and help a child to feel less vulnerable, especially in the scary world of school. Many children I talked to mentioned someone being able and willing to help when they get stuck on their work as an important aspect of friendship, a sign that the pressure to do well is another anxiety a friend can relieve. The motivation to choose someone who is kind or fair or loyal or helpful and reliable can be explained as a self-interested move to ensure survival as well as a sign that children value these qualities in a moral sense.

Different Types of Friends

So, what are the different types of friends that our children might have during their pre–middle school years? In talking

with a host of children, and seeing the relationships of my
own and others' children, here are the various types of
friends I have noticed:

- Imaginary friends
- "Best" friends
- Therapeutic friends
- Younger/older friendships
- "Bad" friends—naughty, nasty, different values, not very
  likeable
- Parents as friends
- Other family as friends
- Pets and animals as friends
- Virtual or cyber friends

Imaginary Friends

In Chapter 1, we saw that imaginary friends are a common
part of early childhood and that many young children use
them as a way to develop and explore themselves as well as
explore friendship. These relationships can be immensely
valuable.

Imaginary friends are rather like plastic credit cards: They
act as a flexible friend and take the waiting out of wanting.
Not only can they can be conjured up at will, but they are
also available to play any game or any part in a game. Pretend play is very beneficial to children's development, and
shared pretend play, in which two children explore situations and contribute jointly to the story, is especially valu-

able. As Judy Dunn, a psychologist who specializes in children's friendships, wrote, "The cognitive capacities that flourish and grow in shared pretend play are those that underlie our ability to communicate verbally, to share ideas and understanding." However, to build a story collaboratively there needs to be another child present, and the two children need to be of similar mind and "get it" in the same way. A like-minded friend may not be readily available when needed, which is where an imaginary friend comes in handy. Being the child's personal creation, this friend will dovetail perfectly into the scenario a child wants or needs to explore. Although this means there won't be another person whose different ideas can add surprises to the story, the imaginary friend may have words and thoughts put into him that would not have emerged otherwise.

Why Imaginary Friends Are Useful

My daughter had two imaginary friends, Inor and Galor, who went with us on vacations and trips and were woven into her play and story writing from the age of three to about six. They started life as her companions, and they later took on new roles. They became the pupils when she was acting the teacher in her school-based fantasy games; they owned the pets that she craved; they were, of course, the guilty party when she did something wrong; and they were even used once to trump her much older brother when she claimed to his assembled friends that Inor and Galor were his ridiculous and still "present" fiction, not hers!

Imaginary friends can also provide company. Theo, age eleven and an only child, told me she had a secret imaginary friend, a girl called Canya, until she was seven. "I'd meet her while taking the dogs out for a walk on my own, in the canyon close to where we lived. I kept her a secret from my mom and dad. They would have thought I was crazy! She was my close friend until my parents divorced and we had to move. I decided to 'leave' her there but she still was in my mind." Christos, age seven, related, "My friend's called Purple. I see him nine days a week." Kieran, also seven, told me his companion lived under his bed. Seven-year-old Kelly spoke of her imaginary friend, Chris: "One day when I was bored at the swings and needed a friend, I made him up. He stays down in the basement when he is not with me."

The most unlikely objects can become imaginary friends. In an admittedly unusual example, a lonely and rather unhappy boy focused on clothing labels.

Aidan, age six, had very few real friends. He had moved about a bit and had already attended two different schools before enrolling at this third one. His imaginary friends were clothing labels, cut out from his own and other classmates' clothes. Each label had an individual identity. He kept them in his classroom drawer and would take them out from time to time to talk to them. He couldn't read the labels, but in his mind the words printed on them were the names that he had given them.

Imaginary friends can also help children explore something they're worried about, through pretend play. Children can extend their experience and have some power and autonomy in a world in which adults reign supreme.

> Thomas, age four, needed to have a minor operation. Quite by chance, he'd recently been given a doctor's set for his birthday. His mother had added a nurse's head scarf made from an old white towel. As the operation approached, Thomas played obsessively with the kit, being the nurse, pretending to take blood from Togo, his imaginary friend, with a plastic syringe, and bandaging the leg of his teddy bear. Fantasy patients and pretending were central to Thomas's ability to work through his worries about the imminent hospital stay.

The choices that children make about what scenario to act out, which character to be, and in which direction to take the story are safe choices because there's no right or wrong option or any chance to make a mistake and be found wanting. In this safe environment, they can find and develop their true emerging self. The imagination used in pretend play also helps to develop a child's moral sense and ability to reflect, to consider what might have happened in a story and what other people feel or might have felt had we behaved differently in a situation.

Do Imaginary Friends Delay Accepting Reality?

When an imaginary friend moves into your home, it's easy to worry about the "lie" of it and whether this flight of fancy means your child will never engage seriously with reality.

You may think it is your job to bring your child down to earth and curb such immature fantasies. If these "flexible friends" hang around for longer than seems comfortable, the greater worry can then be your own social embarrassment— what your friends will think of you if your child continues to inhabit a dream world, talking to people who don't exist. There is, though, no need to worry. Teachers confirm that it is quite normal for children to keep an imaginary friend until they are seven or even eight without impairing their grasp on reality. Researchers have found that even four-year-olds realize that an imaginary friend is not real. And two- and three-year-olds know they are pretending in "let's pretend" games. Pretending is healthy, and at this age it's absolutely safe to encourage it. Teachers reported having no problem accepting the imaginary friend in the classroom for as long as the pupil needed him to be there. They believe these very personal creations perform a function; if a child needs them, it would be almost cruel to either banish them or prick the bubble and assert they are a mistaken fiction. They also pointed out there's not much difference in a child's head between talking to a favorite stuffed animal, which parents are usually happy about, and talking to an imaginary friend.

For How Long Do Imaginary Friends Last?

By the time a child reaches eight years of age, fantasy friends have generally faded. This is also the age when children typically figure out that neither tooth fairies nor Santa Claus exist; until then, children readily believe the unbelievable and enjoy the fantasy, though one teacher said she thought children often hide their fantasy friends rather than grow out of them. Eventually these figments of imagination finally become replaced by a flesh-and-blood genuine best friend.

Best Friends

Almost all children from middle childhood onward like to have a best friend who makes them feel special and especially selected. And sometimes there's pressure on children to have someone they can call a best friend because they often do things in pairs at school. Best friends are important to both boys and girls, although girls may feel more pressure to have one than boys. But what, exactly, is a "best friend," when do children typically identify someone as being a best friend, and what qualities give that relationship special status? How important is it in terms of children's development to have a best friend, and can they have more than one? The answer to the final question is that of course they can. Adults often say they have two or more "best" friends—never "better" friends, though they might refer to their "good" friends. A younger child will often say, "He's my bestest friend!" This suggests that the term *best friend* can apply to more than one person and that this kind of friendship has a rarer quality that only a few people will provide.

We learned earlier that children begin to use the word *friend* sometime between three and four years of age. They begin to describe someone as a "best friend" when they're five or six, but that does not mean they use the term with precision. At this stage it can simply mean they have a close friendship with someone. It is not usually until the onset of middle childhood, at about age eight, that a child will begin to have clear and different expectations for best friends and feel intimate with them. Even then, using the term raises problems for some older children, especially if they have had a bad experience and been let down.

Theo (her chosen nickname), an eleven-year-old American living in London, reflected on her experience with best friends. She said,

> In preschool you can become best friends in just five minutes. Even now, I'm not sure you actually choose your best friend because you have little groups—I have four best friends in one group and a pair, me and Ellie. Best friends can just happen, often through chance. So I have five best friends here in the UK, but not all of them know they're my best friend. They don't know because if someone calls you their best friend it's a bit rude not to call them it back. I don't let them know, then they don't have that worry and responsibility about saying it back to me. And I have another five back home in Los Angeles. We were a little group. One's a boy called Zaq. Most people think boys and girls shouldn't be friends. I see them when I go back, but

it's not so easy now. I have lots of other friends here too. Best friends and good friends are different.

What makes them a best friend? I trust them, most of them. My best friend Heidi doesn't believe in best friends. She thinks they're not fair because people get upset if they're not included. A true best friend, you have to get to know them and for quite a long time, to find out what they're like. Basically, we're in constant communication after school. . . . We're texting or calling each other. We're really close. A best friend is when you're really close and see each other a lot. I used to be best friends with Ellie, too, but Ellie and Heidi were always fighting. I wanted to be friends with both, but their fights meant it didn't work out.

Ten-year-old Aron was similarly tentative about the value of the term *best friend*. "Best friends are just as important for boys. But at my school I think we shouldn't have a best friend because it suggests you also have a worst enemy. That's not helpful. You should just have lots of good friends; just in case you have a fight with your best friend you'd have no one else. I don't have many people who understand me. My biggest friend does. When he isn't there, there are people to play with in the usual group, but it doesn't feel the same." Jodie, age eleven, said, "What's a best friend? They say 'well done' to you. If their mouth stinks you should go and tell them. You're doing it for them, though some think you're cutting them up. Best friends should be able to talk like that."

Yassin, age nine, said, "Gilmaan's my best friend. . . .
He's the kindest boy I've ever met. My friends are very, very
important to me. That's how they be to me." Arman, age
eleven, said of his best friend, "I trust Kaide because he's
been to my house and I go to his." Kelly, age seven, said,
"Jay is my best friend because in first grade he told me about
devils and ghosts and I thought it was interesting and
funny. We both like to tell jokes and funny stories."

Best Friends—Who Says So and What Does It Mean?

Best friend seems to be a label that is bandied around quite a
bit, largely because children want to claim they have one,
often to meet the expectation that they should. For some,
the best friend is very, very special because they feel that
they know each other very well. The "best friend" pairs that
I talked to—both boys and girls—frequently referred to the
length of time they had known one another, implying that
they therefore really understood each other and there was a
particular feeling of intimacy. Arman also said of Kaide,
"He's like my third brother." Some older children had reser-
vations about the term, perhaps because they had been
around long enough to know that even best friends can let
you down.

Reliability and intimacy are clearly important require-
ments in someone who is deemed a best friend, but none of
the children I talked to conveyed any sense of owning or

possessing their best friend. Best friends will not be nasty to you, and they're expected to look out for you, but being a best friend is clearly not seen primarily as an exclusive relationship. Indeed, those asked whether the label *best friend* had to be agreed by each side in order to make it real were adamant that it did not—you could consider someone your best friend but the other person did not have to feel the same way about you, and that was okay. However, Kelly, age seven, thought it best if they did "like each other the same amount as it makes you less likely to boss each other around." Working all this out and coping with knowing that you like someone better than they like you but you both nonetheless like each other is confusing.

TIPS . . . for reassuring a child who has no best friend and is upset

- Explain that most children have a range of different types of friends, and best friends are not necessarily the best kind to have if they lead to jealousy or restrictions.
- Someone may refer to a classmate as a best friend, but it doesn't necessarily mean the friendship is truly special or that the closeness that's felt is mutual.
- A genuine best friendship takes time to find and to build. It's better to wait rather than to scramble to find one quickly and get hurt.
- Encourage your child to identify a friendship he'd like to develop, suggest he might invite that person over, or offer to include him on a family trip, but don't push anything.

Therapeutic Friends

If your child has several good friends, each of these relation-ships is likely to be slightly different and will mesh with a different aspect of her personality or experience. Occasion-ally someone appears on the scene as a good friend who would seem an unlikely choice: someone who has very dif-ferent interests or a very different personality or family background, or someone who is not as kind and reliable as we'd like. Although there may appear to be no obvious rea-son for the attraction, there will often be some underlying connection that neither child is necessarily aware of that explains it. Two children who have just acquired a new baby brother or sister, have parents who argue frequently, have just experienced bereavement, or have a mom or dad who is away from home a lot will often bond together. For example, Shardae, age ten, said of her friend Jodie, "My dad doesn't live with me. Jodie's the same—she understands what it's like."

It was similar for Kate and Lizzie, also age ten. Kate had become increasingly close to Lizzie, who was pretty miserable because her parents had recently split up. Kate feared her parents might also separate as they argued a lot. When Lizzie asked Kate to go along with her to see the school counselor, Kate agreed. Though she never joined in, what she heard gave her the time and the opportunity to think about her own situation, which she said later was very helpful.

Although a child or young person can be comforted by having a friend who will understand her situation without having to explain anything, it is rare for any child under the age of twelve to use a friend to "offload"—that is, as a therapist. There is a difference between *therapeutic* and *therapist*, however. A younger child may not talk about his issues because he sees his life as normal and therefore unremarkable—he will know nothing different. He may also keep it to himself because he doesn't have the vocabulary to describe his feelings—for instance about bereavement, a family argument, or a breakup. Or it may be that what he most values from his friends is normality—something that hasn't changed—to help him have some fun and temporarily forget his problems. Even teenagers will regularly choose to keep family issues private and use friends as a diversion. In this way friends can be of great therapeutic value.

Friends of a Different Age

It is not unusual for a child to become friends with someone who is more than twelve months older or younger than he is. As the great majority of schools are organized by grades that correspond to chronological age, children typically make friends from similarly aged classmates. However, within any class there can be a difference of one year between the youngest and the oldest. If, therefore, a child who is young for her class befriends someone in the year below, the age gap may be similar to a possible same-class friendship. In other words, there is nothing odd about having a friend from the class below, especially as the two children may be better matched emotionally and developmentally.

Out of school, the context for mixing and socializing is often more flexible. In urban settings, for instance, children of various ages often play with each other in communal space, and those who are close neighbors may almost live in each other's homes. Eleven-year-old Neta, an only child, told me, "I also have a home friend called Lizzie. She's nine and more like a younger sister." Neta clearly valued having the attention of someone who stood in for the sister she didn't have—perhaps another example of a friend having therapeutic value. For anyone being teased or picked on at school, the time spent with a younger, less threatening person can recharge confidence and provide emotionally safe playtime.

Psychologists use the term *emotional age* to acknowledge that children of the same chronological age can be more or less mature in emotional terms for that age. Children who are going through a family breakup, who have been ill and temporarily absent from school, or who have moved several times recently can be set back emotionally. While waiting for their confidence to return, they may benefit from having an "easier" relationship with a younger child. If you have the reverse experience, and your child regularly enjoys the company of an older child, he may have been attracted by having a similar interest, or the two might be like-minded in other ways. This is not a problem. However, it is conceivable that the older child is looking for someone to manipulate—or even groom for illegitimate reasons—and so it's wise to monitor the relationship carefully and encourage additional friends closer in age.

"Bad" Friends

"Bad" friends, as we might want to call them, can fall into several groups:

- Those who have a reputation for being naughty and like to live up to it, who could lure your child to follow their bad example into long-term bad ways.
- Those who are not very nice as friends—who can be downright manipulative and unpleasant and cause your child great distress.
- Those growing up with different family values that, if copied, could undermine your influence and authority.
- Friends that you don't like, or the children of your friends that you don't like.

As these four sets of situations are different and require very different understandings and responses, they are treated separately here. Tips for helping you to judge whether friends are leading your child into danger and on how to redirect your child, if you feel this is necessary, are covered in Chapter 5.

Naughty Friends

It is great when our child strikes up a friendship with someone from a family that has similar values and styles to ours. We hear so many stories of children being led astray by others with different agendas—who don't care for school; who are into deviant ways such as smoking, drinking, and vandalism as young as nine or ten; who are rude and loud and enjoy being a nuisance to others. Even quite young children can appear to delight in minor deviance and rule-breaking and can seem set on a no-good path.

Generally, though, parents worry too much and unnecessarily, either because the influence is not as powerful as we feared or because the worrying behavior is short-lived. Don't forget that healthy children need to be naughty. Children love to flirt with danger; flouting rules can be an assertion of independence and self-respect, even power—making some decisions for yourself and not always doing an adult's bidding. It's far easier to be naughty with someone else who then provides a kind of Dutch courage. Being naughty together can also be a way to have fun if a child doesn't know of any other way. All of this sounds, and usually is, harmless. However, there is evidence that children with naughty friends can become more badly behaved the more time they spend together. Even like-minded four-year-olds have been seen plotting to break rules, swearing together, and playing imaginative games that involved violence and stealing. Friends can become a negative influence and lead to a child taking pride in his "troublesome" label. But even then, we should not get overly anxious. A period of conspiratorial mischievous behavior and high spirits does not necessarily mean our child is on the road to ruin.

How to tell if it's going too far . . .

Again, Chapter 5 features a list of behaviors that will help you judge whether things are going too far. Here is a short list of questions to help you pitch your problem appropriately:

- Is he naughty or rude in every situation, or just occasionally?
- Is he endangering himself by defying commonsense safety rules?
- Is he physically or verbally abusive to you or his siblings?
- Do the friends ever do intentional damage to your home?

Bad Friends Who Exploit and Manipulate

Especially when children are young, friendship can involve quite a bit of what adults would call foul play—betrayal, plotting, teasing, and victimization. It is, sadly, quite common for younger children's friendships to be unbalanced and for one or more individuals to exploit the perceived weakness, or niceness, in another. This is rather different from three- and four-year-olds saying, "We don't like you today," but who probably mean, "Today, we'd rather play this game on our own—we'll play with you again tomorrow," but who find that too hard to express fully so they use a clumsy verbal short cut. From the age of about seven or eight, children start to pull rank: They like to see if they can get the upper hand, and what happens if they do. If there is persistent exploitation or someone frequently causes upset and uncertainty, it suggests the relationship is an unbalanced, unhealthy pairing that verges on bullying.

This is what faced Amy, now ten, when she was seven and eight. Her friends were so nasty and her anxiety eventually became so overwhelming that she was physically sick on the playground one lunch break. Amy is now more wary than hurt or bitter.

> I didn't tell anyone it was happening for a long time, I'm not sure why. When I was sick, in my mind I could see Milly's face. She was talking about me to someone else and plotting to pick on me. I was sick on Thursday. She'd invited me to her party which was on the Saturday after, and during the party Millie made sure everyone knew and they all talked about it. It was horrible. This year, though, Milly's really nice to me. I don't know why she's got better. You can still see her strong personality . . . and she doesn't have a best friend anymore 'cuz nobody trusts her. We're friendly but not good friends anymore.

Friends Who Are a Bad Influence

One mom complained to me that her son didn't want to have piano lessons anymore because his friend said learning the piano was silly. Another worried about the unhealthy food that her daughter was eating at her friend's home and the sweets that lay about the kitchen that she could help herself to any time. Another thought her child might get too big-headed going to the rich kid's house and didn't want to feel shown up. Another believed her son's friend was overindulged with far too many toys, which might make her son less tolerant of their simpler lifestyle. These worries are natural.

It would be impossible for a child never to make friends with someone different because no family is identical. These clashes and conflicts can feel threatening, or at least disturbing, but tolerance and openness are important to managing any relationship. Children should be allowed to mix widely to broaden experience and form their own values, and clashes of value or approach provide a useful opportunity to discuss the matter of not being overly influenced by friends. Giving in here and there is unlikely to spell the end of your influence across all areas. And if, for example, you feel you must concede to ending the musical instrument lessons, these could be started again later; consuming the occasional bit of unhealthy food is not unhealthy in the context of a generally balanced diet; and children have to develop self-discipline and not depend on parents to tell them continuously what to do and how to behave. Children are less impressionable than we sometimes think.

Friends You Don't Like

My son's best friend lives close and comes over a lot. About every other visit he wants to go home early. He's quite selfish and a bit weak, and hates to not get his way. I usually call my friend and she comes to get him, and I don't say much. But I don't want my son to see this tactic as a good way to deal with any fallout.—Rosa

When my son was nine he was friendly with Mickie, who . . . was a year older. Mickie wasn't a close friend and went to a different school, but he didn't seem to have many school friends and relied on my son for amusement. He'd . . . expect to come in to join whatever family stuff was going on. He'd also expect to join in with other friends who'd come over to play. If we invited him to eat with us, he'd go home to check what was on offer there, and then choose which food he liked best. He also lied about a lot of things, including whether his parents knew where he was. Most irritating, he'd get upset and flounce off home mid-game or just leave suddenly for no apparent reason—"I'm going now. Bye." I didn't want to cause a scene with his parents, but it was beginning to get me down.—Mary

In both of these situations, the visiting child is trying to retain an edge, or power. It may be irritating, but it is not for you to try to make good any insecurity or to change the child in any way—he's not yours to raise! By mid-childhood, your child will be making his own sense of these encounters and won't necessarily be tempted to try similar tactics. If he wants some support to say no to a visit at any time, you could help with that—but no lies: just, "It's not convenient right now." The mom in the second story found the situation resolved itself naturally when Mickie transferred to middle school, found new friends, and no longer wanted to be seen playing with someone younger. The first mom stopped having to worry when the boys' friendship petered out soon after.

Family as Friends

Families can offer children a great deal of succor, intimacy, and fun across the age range, but the closeness and reliability offered by the majority of families does not mean any particular family member should become a substitute or replacement for a reliable friend.

Parents as Friends

What helps children make and keep friends more readily is having a warm, supportive, emotionally stable, and reliable relationship with a parent in the first months and years of their life, before they develop independent friendships with other children. Psychologists use the term *secure attachment* to describe this kind of relationship. The difference between providing a secure attachment and being a close friend to your child is important. A secure attachment meets a child's first need to feel safe, loved, and reliably cared for and to receive the kind of predictable intimate social and physical attention that develops trust. Trust and reciprocity enable links to be made in the brain that encourage positive and controllable emotional responses rather than uncontrollable and defensive or aggressive ones. Tyler, age five, expressed this in his comment: "My dad's my best friend. At night time we snuggle up. We play games we really like." When a child feels securely attached, she will feel safe, loved, and lovable and have the confidence to separate and explore her independence and build other relationships. However, a parent cannot sculpt a child's individual identity. That task is for the child, through exploring friendships, skills, and personal preferences. Veronica, age eleven, put it very well: "Some parents keep their kids in and won't let them socialize. They don't find out about themselves then."

A parent should not be tempted to think that he or she can take the place of a contemporary as a child's main friend. A parent can provide some of the benefits that a child derives from friendship with someone of a similar age, but not many of them. Parents should offer a home in which a child feels loved and cared for and looked after. This is a very valuable backdrop to happy friendships because confidence and positive self-regard act as a magnet for friends. If a potentially exclusive parent-child friendship is emerging, it's likely to have been molded by the parent to meet a personal need— for approval, companionship, and affirmation. It is therefore rooted in selfishness and, in effect, imposes demands and sacrifices on the child. If you rely on your child to provide you with companionship and entertainment, he may not have the chance to develop true friendships with his peers. A child will pick up that his parent's happiness seems to depend on spending time together, which not only imposes unspoken obligations but also lays a difficult and inappropriate responsibility on the child for his parent's sense of well-being. In effect, the child is being asked to act as a parent to the parent.

Loving and Hating

This is not to say that parents shouldn't be friendly and approachable—of course they should. Hostility is far more damaging to a child than friendship. But children need to love and hate a parent or caregiver as part of their emotional development; they need to be naughty and to challenge and have a safe place to dump frustration and anger without any comeback that threatens their sense of security—the unconditional bit of love that is so important for a parent to provide. They also need private space, private time, and eventually private lives in order to learn to separate and become an individual with a distinct identity. If parents strive to be their children's friends for their own comfort, especially if they have no other close friendships, it can interfere substantially with a child's healthy social and emotional development. Older, nearly adult, children who state, "My mom's my best friend'" are saying something different, perhaps about being able to speak freely and tell all. If, however, they mean that their mom is their sole soul mate, it might predict tensions and conflict when, as an adult, they try to balance competing relationships and commitments. Indeed, they might not feel sufficiently free or separate to make an independent commitment.

Brothers and Sisters as Friends

Some siblings are good friends, others are total enemies, and often they alternate between the two. Some are useful playmates whereas others will be so different in age or will want to play such different games that their existence seems hardly relevant. Mandy, age nine, declared that her brother and sister were her friends, too. Her sister is twenty and her brother, five. It is lovely for her that she gets on well with them both, but neither will be able to give the same support and protection that an on-hand, similar-aged friend will provide. Eleven-year-old Veronica said, "I have four sisters and one brother. Yes, they're like a friend. Your friends are like your family, another family for you. What's the difference? Nothing really different, but . . . you can tell more to your sisters because they won't tell anyone. They're closer to you." However, siblings who are close in age can be a threat. Chloe, age ten, was worried that "my friends are going to like my older sister [age twelve] more than me." Yusra, age eight, said, "I have six brothers and sisters. Are they my friends? No! They're rude. Friends don't come to my house. Friends are important, but family's more." Relationships with brothers and sisters are usually complex. Although siblings may attend the same school, unless they're twins they will not be there to offer support in class or, necessarily, at playtime.

Extended Family as Friends

If someone has a number of cousins, aunts, uncles, grandparents, second cousins, or even great-grandparents and great aunts living nearby, it is understandable that this may reduce a child's need to make close friendships outside the family. A few of the younger children I talked to mentioned a grandmother or cousin as their soul mate. Annie, age six, declared, "Nanny Annie is my special nan. I really love her. She meets me from school. She's my dad's mom." Thalia, age seven, said, "My friends are nice but I love my great-grandma!" The larger the family, the greater the range of personalities a child will encounter. Mixing with everyone can teach a certain amount of tolerance and hands-on experience of moods.

Cousins in the same school or who live close by can also be a great asset—like a sibling but without the rivalry. Said six-year-old Casey, "My cousin Lauren is the person in my family who I really care about." Cousins Georgie and Chris, three months apart in age, lived down the road from each other throughout their childhood. They were very close, and the strengthened sense of family they gave each other helped them to be more confident in their other relationships. However, it could be significant that these highly protective relationships were mentioned only by the younger children who are still finding their way around the minefield that is the school playground.

Emma, age eleven, who is an only child but close to several cousins, admitted, "It's hard to be best friends with a cousin. You can get very close but it never gets intimate, like with a best friend. I have two friends at school in the same years who are cousins, and they hate it. Cousins can be very different from you. It's nice being close because when you spend time with them you can really enjoy the time more. You know what to say, you don't feel as shy. You're not scared your cousin is going to judge you, and you'll always make up." It seems that until a child can feel safe in a personal and proven friendship, family bonds can be highly supportive and beneficial. However, some experience of the rougher aspect of friendship is useful, particularly to help them judge people sensibly and develop a healthy skepticism—an attitude that will provide good instincts in other situations, for instance when surfing the Internet.

Virtual/Cyber Friends

The typical American child spends, in an average week, as much time using media outside school as he spends on work in school. American children age eight years and older spend an average of close to seven hours a day using media, most of which is televiewing, in front of a screen. Whereas children used to communicate with friends out of school by talking on the phone and more recently by texting, they now increasingly use social networking sites and chat rooms to continue their relationships during vacations, on the weekends, and after school. Virtual friendships—friendships forged with other people whom they have not met—are another increasing feature of the lives of children older than twelve (a topic that falls outside the scope of this book). However, many eight- and nine-year-olds are beginning to use chat rooms and networking sites such as Facebook to converse with their school friends, and they may start to explore further afield. When I asked eleven-year-old Aron whether he chatted to his friends on the computer, he retorted, "No! When I use the computer I just go onto websites and play games." Yet nine-year-old Hannah confirmed that she goes online after school to chat, as did her classmate Jamie, also nine.

What are the lessons and guidelines for parents of children under twelve who are going online to MySpace or Facebook? Can virtual friends offer the same emotional rewards and learning opportunities as real friends? How worried should you be if your child has a hundred or more virtual friends online yet spends no time meeting and socializing, or indeed chatting online, with anyone from her local area or peer group at school?

There are different views on this. In any case, it may be too early for there to be any clear answers from research about the longer-term impact. Intuition and common sense will help to assess whether a child has a balanced attitude or whether he might be overly preoccupied with the tally of *virtual* friends he has, spending too much time in chat rooms or on networking sites and not enough time developing friendships in the real world. Some believe that virtual friends are unhelpful because they encourage children to indulge in fantasy and wishful thinking about who they are and to "doctor" their persona to correct aspects of themselves that they'd rather hide. In the chat room they can introduce themselves as they want to be. They can control their self-image and even invent it, and perhaps then become used to living a world of lies.

Of course, the same danger lies in the other direction: Your child can be playing straight while the other person is fabricating an identity to cultivate a friendship. (Ways to counter stranger danger and online bullying are discussed at the end of Chapter 6.) The healthiest relationships exist when people feel equal and are confident about being accepted despite any weaknesses. There is no substitute, according to this view, for real conversation and watching faces and bodies at the same time as talking to take in and interpret one's body language. Only a face-to-face friendship can generate genuine empathy and tolerance, the hallmarks of a close friendship.

Others, however, believe that virtual friendship can be the start of a real friendship; that virtual friendship creates more possibilities and can bring people together in vastly different circumstances and parts of the world. One adult advocate said, "These global friendships give me the chance to reach people who are not necessarily like me. This new friendship is amazing. It can help people to open up because they feel safe from gossip. For some, it's the real world that can't be trusted and is fake."

These are the views of adults. We need to remember that our children are just that—children, not adults—and that they need to learn the basics of face-to-face relationships in order to have a real choice about how they satisfy and balance their emotional needs and variable relationships in the future. But the Internet is a fact of life. It can be good for a shy or quiet child to crystallize his personality and develop communication skills that will improve general confidence. Within a controlled educational environment, it can be, and is being used to link children across the world or in different parts of the country to exchange views, life stories, and knowledge. It can also usefully connect your child to the school or to classmates for easy access to project or homework information and connect him to others outside school with the same interests and hobbies.

Popularity and Friendship

Popularity is not the same as friendship, though most children fail to realize this and spend at least some time during their childhood bemoaning their lack of popularity. Some will feel like a failure because they're not even in the outer circle of the current popular class star. A child who feels "out of it" will either go all-out to become the center of attention—the popular one—or, more commonly, try to join the in-crowd to bask in the "sunshine kid's" reflected glory. Joe, about to move on to middle school, said he'd try to identify the class joker when he arrived and make him his friend. "People always want to be friends with the jokers, so I'll be in with the popular crowd," was his comment. In one class, a talented young soccer player who had been spotted by a scout was the hero almost all the other boys worshiped—to the point that, as a teacher remarked, even the brainiest boy felt a failure and lost faith in himself.

The elementary school teachers that I talked to agreed that *popularity* is tricky to define. "The person who is popular may not be the one with most friends—quite the opposite, in fact," one elementary school teacher said. "He'll never have one special, main friend because he just plays with everyone. You can tell quite early on in their school life who is going to

▓ TIPS . . . for if your child feels outside the popular circle

- Empathize with what she could be feeling—inferior because she's not getting as many party invites as the popular girls; dissatisfied with who she is, because she wants to be like someone else; ignored, because she wants the popular girl to take more notice of her.
- Tell her what your experience was as a child—"I *so* remember feeling on the outside like you seem to!"
- Point out the advantages she has—"You've got three really great friends whom you have such a good time with. Paula, Sasha, and Michelle stand by you and wouldn't like to feel they're not good enough in your eyes."
- Encourage her to be herself and not to try to change at all just to gain favor—"You're just great as you are. It's not good to try to be someone you're not just to get noticed—like, selling your soul to be popular."
- Reassure her that friendship comes in lots of shapes and sizes—one's not better than the other.

be the most popular child in the top class. The individual is almost always quite independent, happy to stand out slightly and never strives to fit in, because he doesn't need to. He or she is always happy to be different, confident, often has a spark in the eye, works hard—and he won't bother so much what others think of him. He'll have charisma." The quality that this description highlights is *acceptability*, which is different from friendship in one important way. Friendship necessarily involves a two-way flow of interest and involvement, whereas acceptance and popularity are narrower, one-way, and one-sided concepts—the person is liked, but he or she does not have to like everyone back.

So, whereas the usual understanding of popularity is "having lots of friends" the teachers consider it closer to "likeable"—a free spirit, an attractive personality who commands attention and is admired and respected. This is rather different from someone who has an impressive number of friends. Children who want friends understandably believe that the more they have, the better. But totaling up friends misses the point. As children use friends to gain relationship skills in preparation for their future complex adult relationships—intimate relationships with partners, spouses, and children as well as looser networks in the neighborhood or in the workplace—having a few close friends is likely to teach them more than gaining the general regard of most of the class.

3

WHY FRIENDS MATTER,
AND WHEN THEY DON'T

It is very easy for us to underrate the importance of our children's friends. It can be hard not to become irritated when you continually have to accommodate one particular child's friend and easy to trivialize the hurt when their friendships end or go wrong. On the other hand, we can become far too anxious if our child lacks a full bevy of friends or doesn't want to have anyone over to play. The way most parents typically try to learn more about what's going on is to ask questions. We may try to inquire casually and neutrally, but often our inquiries are so transparent that our child quickly detects we're anxious, which may make him think that he has a problem when he doesn't. This chapter describes why friends matter so much to most children and why, despite this, some equally well-adjusted children might be less needy of friends and comfortable with one or two. I'll also suggest what you can say or do in a range of situations to ensure your child feels understood by you rather than undermined.

Why Friends Are Important for Children

Looking at a room full of friends she had accumulated since the age of five who were assembled to celebrate her twenty-first birthday, Maria said, "To all my friends here, thank you, you've helped me grow."

From early on, friends help young children to develop socially and emotionally, which enables them to grow into well-rounded, sociable, balanced, adaptable, and caring adults. More than that, though, friends help to make you who you are. Friends are like tree rings, laid down inside us over the years. They mark key moments in our life, and once in place they can never be erased. The thicker rings represent the significant friends who made a strong impact when we particularly needed them, perhaps during a personal upheaval or a developmental moment when our identity was crystallizing and our confidence fast forwarding. Through the understanding, love, or security offered, the fun they provided, and the interests and perspectives they brought with them, these key friends define each of us: They represent our origins and signpost our story. They leave an impression inside each of us, even if they don't stay around forever.

Friends are also essential to children because they accept and understand each other as they actually are. Families aren't so good at this. Parents can be too pressed to see and to respond to the personality of each of their children; they can be too biased, believing their child can do no wrong, or more focused on the person they want their child to be. At home, children can get locked into roles—the baby of the family or the difficult and demanding one. Friends release children from any family preconceptions and provide the opportunity for their personalities to develop freely.

The following sections look closely at the advantages of friendship and explain how friends can be significant to much younger children.

Familiarity and Security

The biggest benefit of friendships to very young, preschool children is in providing familiarity and security, which, naturally, also contributes to well-being and social adjustment. Seeing a particular child in the same place at a similar time can become part of the rhythm, pattern, and comfort of life, providing the familiarity that helps them to feel safe in the world. This is why some childcare professionals suggest young children fare better with simple, consistent care rather than a part-time mix that may be confusing and involve too many children, adults, and changes to enable familiarity and a sense of security to take root.

For older children, familiar friends can be an important lifeline during times of change and difficulty. Not only do they act as the secure tethering point when other things in their lives are changing—starting a new school; moving; coping with family changes such as the birth of a new sibling, acquiring step-siblings, or having a parent move out. Friends also help to shore up confidence and self-esteem, which are inevitably threatened during times of stress and uncertainty. If you know your friends are still there for you, you can cope with so much more.

Learning Through Friendship

Children can learn good things and bad things from their friends. On the positive side, they learn how to get along together and pick up or share new interests and skills, and they can explore further afield in the protective company of others. On the negative side, children can pick up "bad" ways of behaving and talking, and bad attitudes toward teachers, schoolwork, or authority.

Friends are particularly important to only children because they teach them things that other children will often learn from their siblings or larger family group activities. When friends come over, you might suggest they play a board game, and even join in if you feel it's suitable.

Children are famously honest. Almost every parent I have known has commented at some point on the directness and near cruelty of their child's dealings with others— even with their friends. Parents tend to be masters of tact and manipulation, of positive feedback and praise; but, more important, we are very protective of our children and hate to hurt them or see them hurt. We've also learned that it can sometimes be counterproductive to speak our minds because it can backfire, and we certainly have to choose our moment carefully when we do. So it's puzzling that a child will tolerate something that we would blanch at or say something unpleasant to someone she calls a friend.

TIPS . . . to help your young child make friends and be sociable

- Try to make and maintain a friendship network while your child is young so she regularly meets others of a similar age. Meeting other babies is less important during the first year (though your sanity may benefit!) but any contact from birth on will help her to be relaxed with other children and to open up to them. Local children's centers often organize informal drop-ins, small group coffee sessions, or weekly storytimes to bring children together when socializing isn't the focus. These are useful first steps in forming a loose circle of contacts. But even having a cup of tea with a neighbor will help a child to develop a mental picture of what communication and friendship entails.

- Children do, of course, watch their moms and dads socializing. They pick up a great deal about the value of friends and how to communicate in a friendly and confident way simply from being in the same room when you are chatting and laughing. Take your child with you, if you can, when you go to meet friends, and make friendly, light conversation part of your family's usual behavior.

- If your child attends a daycare center, watch carefully for any sign that your child has a favorite playmate. See if you can coordinate with that child's parents for play dates outside of daycare.

- Talk warmly and approvingly about that child, referring to him by name.

- Try to keep your children's friendships going when they face any changes they could find unsettling. For example, invite previous friends over on the weekend if your child starts a new school and knows no one else who is going.

- Accept that during any stressful time, which could include tests and exams, children need their friends more, even though you may think friends could be an unwelcome diversion from the task!

But the beauty of good friends is that they can be tough and tender, and older children pay more attention to them than they do to you. Tough talk in the context of a tender relationship of mutual trust allows friends to tell it straight, so the message hits home. Parents who constantly criticize a child get tuned out and ignored, and constant praise can be equally sifted and rejected—it doesn't sound honest. Status-conscious siblings are typically nasty and overcritical, so they can't be trusted to provide measured and objective feedback either. Friends let a child know how he impacts them and give him the chance to change. That's how children learn.

Having Fun

The young of all mammals are extremely playful. Puppies, kittens, lion cubs, bear cubs, and children all love to bundle and pounce. They are pre-programmed to be playful because play helps them to learn so much and be all-around healthy as well as to practice things they'll need to do as an adult. All this is designed to be achieved while having fun. Play definitely cheers up human children and can help them to forget any difficulties or sadness, for a while at least. A child can play by himself and be absorbed, but as he grows older, by around the age of six, he'll need to play with people of a similar age if he is to have side-splitting fun, test the boundaries, explore more of his possible self, and develop his sense of humor, imagination, and physical strength.

Children love to laugh and giggle—at anything, and often at nothing at all except at others giggling. They love to be amused. Allana said about Sacha, "I like her because she's really funny!" Jessie, age two, laughed as she said of her good friends, "I really like them so much. Demetrios cries and then they give him time out and then they give him a dreidel and the dreidel makes him laugh." Older children will tend to gravitate to someone who has a similar sense of humor. Lyndie, age six, said, "Becky finds the same things funny as me. We giggle lots." Esme, age five, beamed when she exclaimed, "I really love having fun!" Children probably enjoy laughing together not just because of the "happy" chemicals that are produced in the brain during laughter but also because laughter creates a shared, intimate moment in which children can feel close to each other and therefore safe. Very few people turn nasty in the middle of having a good time!

Pretend Play

You don't have to crack up laughing in order to have fun: At all ages, children can have great fun together creating a world of make-believe. Pretend play is particularly important once children start in preschool, but a child can be introduced to pretend play from very young. Your eighteen-month-old will love to do things like sit in a cardboard box and turn it into a spaceship; two-year-olds will enjoy making a hat out of a pair of shorts; or three-year-olds may eat a biscuit in a way that it takes on the shape of a moon. Children enjoy seeing their food looking like a face, with different pieces representing the eyes, nose, and mouth. They'll recognize it and realize it is possible to pretend that something is something else. When you make animal sounds, they learn that it is possible to pretend to be an animal, which they can eventually copy. When a one- or two-year-old child looks at a simple book with beautiful illustrations, he may not be able to follow the words, but he can gaze into the picture and see something he never sees in his daily life—he will dwell on it and take in visual possibilities that will extend his potential imagination and story-making.

As already stated, pretend play contributes to children's healthy development. At nursery school my son used to dress up with his "girl friend" and get married, swapping roles as bride and then groom. Nursery teachers don't need reminding that cloaks, hats, saucepans, and cardboard boxes fuel imagination and encourage shared pretend play. Later on, and well into their mid teens, boys can play endless card and computer-based or laser war fantasy games with friends, taking on various mystical and mythical personae in battles of strength and wit and no doubt saving maidens in distress as well, sometimes dressing up for their parts. Computer games can also provide opportunities to create and develop more domesticated stories in an alternative family.

Although parents can join in pretend play and take on imagined roles, they tend not to because it feels strange. Friends are more likely to be on the same wavelength and have similar issues they need to examine—the same fears, curiosities, or pleasures; their ideas will dovetail better, and the play will remain essentially childlike and theirs.

Helping Children Develop a Separate Identity

Children need some private space, whether in their head, their bedroom, a corner of the yard, or walking to school alone. Playing with friends away from adult monitoring and interference provides more of that private territory. You know less about what they do at someone else's house than what they do at your home. As children gain the confidence and maturity to become more independent, friends help them to play outside and wander more widely but still safely, to devise plans, cook up secrets, and otherwise conspire against parents in a mild and healthy way as they learn to separate and become more self-reliant.

Children need this time away from parents' prying eyes to become responsible and to feel trusted. One mom I knew used to eavesdrop on her child when she was playing with friends in her bedroom through the baby alarm system, which was still plugged in even though her daughter was now ten. She still used the alarm, she said, to hear a possible asthma attack during the evening as her daughter was prone to them, but she could have unplugged it for the daylight hours. She chose not to because she wanted to hear what they were saying and doing, but in fact she was intruding on her child's privacy and confusing that all-important boundary between parent and child, and mother and daughter in particular. Another mom used to peek at her son through the school playground fence at lunchtime. She wanted to see how he played, and if he played with friends or was on his own. She also believed that she needed to catch a glimpse of him during the day because she missed him so much. If you live very near your child's school it must be quite tempting to sneak a look, but it's not at all helpful to your child if he sees you at it! Parents can and should offer their child increasing autonomy at home, but the taste of real freedom will and must come through friends.

Gaining Experience and Confidence

Especially when they begin to "find their own feet," children use friends to try themselves out. It is a vital time for exploration and skill development, and friends often introduce them to new activities.

When Molly was ten, for instance, she summoned the courage to sing in the school choir, but only because her friends took the plunge with her at the same time. "My friends have made me much more confident," she admitted. Later that year she felt confident enough to try out for a singing part in a school play, which she got, and which could never have happened without that initial push. Jenny, age seven, enrolled in dance class solely because her friend was going, and her friend started because her bigger sister was an old hand there. In another example, a boy joined a soccer club with a friend when he was nine years old, and three years later traveled to the Netherlands with the team.

Desperate for more freedom, nine-year-old Emma was allowed to go to the park without her parents, but only in the company of three particular friends whom her parents trusted. They were even allowed to walk there and back via a disused train track, provided they were back home by the agreed time. Emma felt far more trusted and responsible after this and immediately stopped being so argumentative at home. One thirteen-year-old interviewed for a documentary television program on overprotected children complained with great insight and sadness, "I can't complete my future like this, not being able to go out anywhere." His father didn't even trust friends enough to allow him out as part of a group. Children *need* to have free time away from parents with their friends, kept appropriate to their age and maturity. A "good" family, according to one child, is one "that cares but gives you some freedom and trusts you."

TIPS . . . for how to ensure safety in numbers

It's possible that children are more likely to take silly risks in a large group of friends—the herd mentality can take hold. To keep your child safe, consider taking the following steps:

- Personally select no more than four friends and only involve children whose parents you know and who are, as far as you can know, sensible and trustworthy.
- Keep the first trip focused on a single activity, such as swimming. More open-ended trips to the park can be allowed once children have demonstrated reliability and common sense.
- Make sure you have clear rules—about their route, exactly where they can go, what they can do there, calling in times if they have a cell phone, and an agreed time by which to start their return home and an arrival time.

Acceptance and Identity

From the start of middle childhood around age eight, friends are usually central to a child if he is to feel accepted and acceptable as the individual person that he is. At the start of a child's life, family are usually the main providers of well-being and security through their unconditional love and approval. Later, upon starting school, he will have his sense of acceptability confirmed more generally by being surrounded by groups of friendly peers—being played with, smiled at, welcomed, and included in activities such as group playground games and parties. By age seven or eight he will be more discriminating, needing to test his acceptability and identity through having particular, personal friends who he believes are like him. The role of parties is often eclipsed by sleepovers—especially for girls—which now seem to symbolize the more intimate, personal, shared, and even private nature of these relationships.

It is only when children have reached the age and stage of knowing better who they are—seeing themselves as a distinct person and personality with their culture and gender acknowledged—that identity enters the frame and they use friends to confirm this.

Widening Social and Moral Horizons

Chapter 7 looks in detail at the variety of social, communication, and listening skills children need in order to make and keep friends, and suggests ways you can encourage these at home. But one advantage of friendship is that it can hone these skills once the basics are present. Being able to listen, hear, and respect other people's views and needs helps children keep their friends and learn more from and about them; they learn on the job, so to speak.

Friends therefore widen children's moral and social horizons in ways that families cannot. Friends and their families will have different ways of doing things, different interests and talents, different styles of humor and conversation, alternative food and eating patterns, different likes and dislikes. Through friends, children learn how other people live and can see they need not be threatened by difference. They discover that there are messy homes and tidy homes, homes with food available all the time and homes with it closed away. Nine-year-old Nathaniel's best friend is Mansur, an Iraqi boy in his class. He clearly loves his friend dearly, and they could hardly let go of each other when Mansur returned from a long trip back home, during which Nathaniel moped and fretted about his friend's safety. He reflected on his friendship: "It's good to have a friend from a different culture because you learn about their ways. It's very interesting!"

Children can develop their awareness of others who are less fortunate than they are through hearing of and becoming involved in a friend's personal charitable commitment—a charity often supported by the friend's family. By becoming involved in a fund-raising event and helping to campaign on a charity's behalf, or by joining a youth organization that encourages its members to become aware of disadvantage, children can meet new friends and make closer bonds with existing ones.

⠿ TIPS . . . for making more and closer friends through charity events

- Offer to help make homemade lemonade and set up a stand to sell it to neighbors or in school at recess, donating the proceeds to a selected charity.
- Help your child and a friend host a fund-raising breakfast and invite children who attend a local special-needs school.
- Suggest your child join or co-organize a local charity walk.
- Prepare a joint talk for a school class on a topic that two or more friends care about.
- Introduce your child to Cub Scouts or Girl Scouts, or a similar group, as such clubs can encourage friendships and foster social awareness.

Moral sense develops in several ways: One of these is by becoming sensitive to the feelings and reactions of others so a child learns to imagine what the consequences of his own actions might be and can therefore take responsibility for this. Another is by learning what is right and wrong, or, indeed, how different people may have different views on this. Moral awareness and sensitivity are prerequisites for forming a personal moral code. A child who remains socially isolated or self-absorbed will find it more difficult to imagine himself in other people's shoes.

When Having No Obvious Friend Does Not Matter—And Why You Shouldn't Worry

Though many children will yearn for friends, especially from the age of seven or eight, each child is different and will mature at a different pace. Some children simply seem less bothered about having an identifiable special friend, happy either to spend time on their own or to mix with several friendship groups without a clear "home base" in any one. If your child appears to be either a self-contained "happy-to-be-alone-er" or a comfortable "everyone's-my-friend-er" there is no need to worry. We all know adults who are magnetically drawn to company, sometimes to a dysfunctional extent because they seem unable to exist without scores of people around them; and we know others who would always prefer a quiet evening in to a party or other social gathering. Everybody is different, and there is a great range of habit, practice, and preference among people.

We often need reminding that children are as varied and complex as adults. No child is like another, even in the same family, and none will precisely fit to a pattern of standard development throughout childhood. They will have sociable times and quieter times, confident periods and more wobbly periods. When I called up a friend who is an educational psychologist and the mother of four children to ask about her professional and personal experience of children's friendships, she immediately answered, "Complexity is the nature of your child. You should always take that into account. And so much is in your genes. The son who had the most difficulties making friends had his vulnerabilities from the start. He came out that way!" For adults, sociability has become part of their personality. With children, sociability also reflects three other things: maturity, emotional steadiness, and self-confidence, all of which need time to develop and may ebb and flow in response to challenges and events that make them unhappy.

If your child is holding back from a close commitment, it may be her instinctive way to fine-tune or rebuild confidence or to allow her current troubles to settle before she returns to the friendship fray. Her need to be a bit withdrawn and quiet is more likely to be temporary than a sign of longer-term difficulties. This is well within the range of normal development, so it's probably best to leave things alone and not probe the whys and wherefores unless these are clear and evident. More obviously problematic friendship patterns are looked at in Chapter 5.

A child may have less need for a particular or special friend when he

- is young, either chronologically or emotionally, and is not quite ready for the rough and tumble of friendships.
- is well liked and generally accepted by everyone, regardless of his age.
- needs his parents and family more, perhaps having had an emotional setback.
- has very different passions and interests from the usual, is very self-contained and confident and either

finds other children immature or dull or needs less affirmation.

We'll look at each of these situations in turn.

A Child Is Young, Chronologically or Emotionally

Younger children will enjoy the company of friends but will not need them in the same way that many older children will. Seven-year-old Sacha enthusiastically declared that to her, "friends are very, very important, and family is very, very important, especially my little sister who I really love." She had no problem in considering both friends and family as essential to her happiness, but she would not have been able to express the same sentiment as Selin, four years older, that without her friends "I'd feel like nothing."

When they start school at age four or five, many children are not at all focused on making friends. Home is where their heart and comfort are. Making friends with other children on the school playground takes a great deal of confidence and some very sophisticated social skills, and at the start they may not possess the attributes to find their way in. For a child to enjoy and manage recess, he must be able to:

- not be intimidated by the noise of large numbers of bigger children rushing around
- play the games that are typical of playgrounds everywhere
- discuss and cooperate with others, sometimes in advance, about what to do

- in a simple way, negotiate and agree what to do
- befriend someone who is on his own, or assume he will be accepted by a group he wants to join.
- approach a group confidently and have the words to invite himself into an ongoing game
- occupy himself comfortably if he is on his own
- hide his hurt pride or say the right thing when he is being teased or excluded
- judge the difference between accidents, playful teasing, and fighting and intentionally hostile acts—and respond appropriately

It takes great confidence, courage, and maturity to do all these. When faced with any new situation, it is quite normal for a child to spend a great deal of time watching in order to learn the ropes. Although it can be very upsetting to hear that your child has spent all of recess alone, he will often be happy to be so. It may be more helpful to him to spend some time watching and evaluating other children at play than to join in the highly organized playground activities that schools increasingly offer to prevent some from being on their own. The rather different issue of shyness is addressed in Chapter 5.

A Child Is Liked and Widely Accepted

Some children are content if they feel generally accepted by the group they mix with. They don't seem to need an identifiable relationship with a personal friend. Some friendship

When he was six years old, Hassan was able to join his elder brother and cousin at a weekly children's activity club run by parents. He had been before with his mom many times while dropping off his brother and had sometimes stayed a little while to watch the proceedings, so it wasn't strange to him. The session always started with the twenty-five or so children sitting in a large circle, hearing about the planned program and talking about the week that had passed. No one was made to speak. It was very relaxed. Nonetheless, in the beginning Hassan could not bring himself to join the circle. He would hover in the corridor just outside the main door into the hall and fidget about, half looking in but half not, perhaps fearing that he'd catch one of the adult leaders' eyes and be pressed to sit down. He wouldn't join in any of the noisy team games or other quieter activities either. Even when his own mom was taking her turn at running the session, he hung back. This went on for six weeks. Eventually, he sat in the circle next to his female cousin, but still he played no games. It took him another two weeks to assimilate fully. His reluctance was not a sign of future problems mixing with other children, as he soon had plenty of friends. He was simply not quite ready, not quite confident enough. He wanted to bide his time and decide for himself when he was ready to join in.

researchers see acceptance as the stage before forging firm individual friendships. If they are correct, your child may be taking a little longer to reach the intimate friendship stage, or she may have reverted to being content with this typically younger pattern if she has had an emotional setback. Others, though, would describe an older child who is, and is happy to be, widely accepted and liked as "popular," for a popular child appears to have more confidence and doesn't seek status, approval, or superiority in any particular pairing.

A Child Needs His Parents and Family More, Perhaps After an Emotional Setback

We have seen how managing friendships at school can be very hard work, especially when children are in their "is it on or off today?" phase and they don't know where they stand from one day to the next. There's so much to negotiate and agree on. It is therefore understandable that if a young child feels particularly insecure, she won't have the confidence or stamina to cope as well as usual with friendships. Children can regress in the face of major, or even minor, change: The four-year-old starting school begins to need his comfort blanket or toy more; getting to know a new caregiver may make a child more clingy with a mom or dad; the arrival of a baby brother or sister can make a toddler want a bottle again; or if a father moves out, a child who is beginning to talk can become mute for a time. The same regressive pattern can be evident with friendships. If anything happens at home to disturb the familiar routines and relationships, a child could feel safer by regressing and becoming more dependent on the more secure features of his life rather than his unreliable friends.

But the pattern may not be quite that straightforward. Older children can't regress to babyhood; if they are disturbed and upset, they are more likely to shun invitations and stay put at home, spending more time hanging around you or—more worrying—shut away in their bedroom, resisting attempts to join in family games or meals; or they might form a friendship with a younger child whom they'll find less threatening. There's an inconvenient conundrum about friends—when you're feeling down you need them more, but when you're down and feeling especially vulnerable that's when you handle situations badly, perhaps demand too much to gain reassurance, and are therefore more likely to annoy and lose friends. When a child is settled and confident, making and keeping friends will be no problem. When confidence is low, it is so much harder to make the approaches required—"Are you playing tag again today—can I play?"—stand up for himself and not take clumsy off-the-cuff comments as a personal slight. Spending time with a reliable,

⠿ TIPS . . . for how you might reassure your child

- Say clearly that if things seem to be tougher with friends at the moment, or he's feeling less sociable, it's not surprising—because everyone feels less sure about most things when big changes happen around him. You do, too.
- Reassure him that it's sure to be just a phase while everything settles—that it won't last. People don't change that easily, so his old self will come bouncing back before very long.
- Don't comment negatively on your child's chosen tactic to gain greater personal comfort. Support her while the need is evident.
- Do suggest that he invite a close, reliable friend over and plan something active and fun for them to do.

close friend can help a child to have fun, keep at least something in his life normal, and take his mind off problems.

A Child Has Very Different Interests from the Usual and Either Finds Other Children Immature and Dull or Is Very Self-contained

A child who is very bright will be in advance of his peers intellectually if not emotionally. It is very typical for a youngster who is considered gifted—in the top 2 to 5 percent of the ability range—to have soaked up a huge number of facts about this or that and be passionate, to the point of obsessed, about one or two particular areas. Gifted and talented children can be very imaginative and curious to the point of irritation, insistent in their questioning and demanding of the company they keep. Having possibly been an early and avid reader, he may be used to spending time alone living "in his head," concocting schemes and plans for this electrical circuit or that scientific or nature project. He will often prefer the company of parents and teachers who can field his questions to that of his peers, who will consider him a bit of a freak or a nuisance. It could be hard to find someone to be a friend who is like-minded or as interesting as an adult.

This story illustrates that not wanting to mix much with school friends need not be a problem or suggest later problems, if your child is otherwise fulfilled and happy. By middle school, the curriculum for all children becomes more ambitious and challenging and the differences between children even out. But it would be wise for you to encourage peer

Three-year-old John, the only son of two Polish parents, was obsessed with motorized lawn mowers. He knew all the different manufacturers, the model names and the engine capacity of each, knew how these had changed over the years and even tried to detect differences in engine noises among his neighbors' machines. As a result of this and other obsessions he developed an attention to detail that made him a skillful observer of objects and a terrific draftsman a few years later, having spent so much of his time alone and thus able to draw endlessly and improve his skill. While still in grade school, he drew buildings in detail and then moved onto naval ships of every shape and size, being precise about the number and position of deck guns, for example. By the age of eight he had become passionate about insects and other small creatures, kept a vivarium for his pet reptiles, and had mice, cats, rabbits, and every other animal he could persuade his parents to let him keep. John had plenty of parental attention, and his collection of animals seemed to take the place of friends. He had always seemed to be very grown-up, having been used to so much adult company and knowing so much. He didn't gel with his classmates, largely because he wasn't interested in having anyone home who couldn't relate to his passions, but he didn't feel isolated or depressed about this. In fact, he had a very clear sense of belonging (to the Polish community) and a clear picture of his identity. He met his few friends at the riding stables and the local cub scout pack.

When he moved to middle school, he found more to do and more like-minded boys and adjusted and fit in well.

friendships, nonetheless. If school isn't the right place for your child to strike a satisfying friendship, perhaps an outside club can provide a more selective group. It is just possible that underneath the self-containment, an unhelpful fear of social situations could take root. It may feel great to have a genius as an offspring, but even geniuses will usually prefer company if it is with like-minded people.

Many children who are educated at home are able to follow their interests and also grow up grounded and confident. The head teacher of a middle school confirmed this for me. She remarked that the handful of children who had been home-educated up to the age of eleven who had come to her school were noticeably confident and more mature than the other incoming students and they had no problem fitting in and making friends. They were certainly not isolated and depressed. The opportunity to make decisions about their life and get to know their true selves and capabilities seems to help to build confidence despite not having had a large number of friends to tell them every day that they were okay.

TIPS . . . for encouraging a self-contained child to become more sociable

- Find out if there is a children's club in the area that specializes in any of your child's passions: science, drama, art, chess, sports, etc.
- Find an online group of children who may have a similar outlook—the National Association for Gifted Children has an independent Children and Youth area on its website for children over the age of three to swap notes with each other and play games. It is available to children worldwide.
- Contact the school or class teacher to check whether your child's outlook, attitudes, or limited need for friends appears problematic. If they see no problems, you probably have no need to worry, though teachers are not infallible.

4

OIL AND WATER

Boys' and Girls' Friendship Patterns

Most parents who have both sons and daughters are very clear about the differences between them, including how they relate to their friends. The differences start early. Boy babies are, on average, more active in the womb, wigglier once born, and seek their caregiver's attention more often than girl babies through limb movements and noises. In general, boys find it harder to sit still, like their life noisy and action-packed, and enjoy facts and action rather than fiction and talking; girls tend to have more patience, love little things and detail, are more reflective from an earlier age, and are more interested in stories and people. Experienced teachers say they fine-tune their praise, targets, and feedback to take into account gender to ensure they get the best from all their pupils.

However, children don't always fit the mold and may be teased as a result. There are boisterous girls and sensitive boys; boys who hate sports and girls who love it; girls who relish getting muddy and boys who are fastidious and insect phobic. And there are others who behave out-of-role in one sphere but conform absolutely to type in another. The same is true of their friendships. Nevertheless, it is useful to generalize and describe patterns and styles of interaction that will be seen in the typical school playground or household on a typical day the world over. As a parent you won't necessarily know whether the behavior you see is absolutely normal for a boy or girl of that particular age or a result of that child's personality and particularity. This chapter explores boys' and girls' friendships through the ages and stages. It looks at the key differences between boys and girls and how this affects their friendships, and at the influence of play styles on friendship patterns; it ends with a review of how to respond if your child encounters problems because he or she doesn't conform to the gender stereotype.

How Boys and Girls and Their Friendships Differ

Despite greatly differing cultures and experiences across the world, children's friendships are similar and change in similar ways at roughly the same age everywhere. This is because they are linked to developmental stages that apply universally.

Ages and Stages of Gender Awareness

Children first have a sense of their gender at around the age of two. For a few years, they experience this more as a superficial self-description similar to hair or skin color, which doesn't go deep and certainly doesn't divide them from one another. They are all children together and are happy to play alongside each other. At break time at preschool, groups of girls and boys will often be seen playing happily both in mixed and in same-gender groups. Back in the school room, though, researchers have noticed that given a choice, children will often prefer a same-sex play partner for one-on-one play, and they will tend to talk about different things to each other.

This peaceful coexistence doesn't last for very long. As we've seen, by the age of seven or eight, and certainly by age nine, girls and boys have become more sensitive about and more loyal to their gender, largely because this is the time all children recast their identity and accept their gender as a defining feature. They seem to take on the stereotypical characteristics of their gender, and a strong us-and-them divide develops. It seems that they need to keep their distance from each other while working things out because inside they still feel similar, which is confusing. Only when their hormones kick in to clarify their differences, and they feel thoroughly comfortable with their new identity, will girls and boys be able to get back together: a clear case, then, of opposite magnetic poles attracting! In other words, during middle childhood, boys and girls are simply exploring what it means to be male or female and exaggerating the various characteristics of their gender as they try each of them out for size. So if you are worried that your daughter has become a pea brain, obsessed with painting her nails, following boy bands, or creating hairstyles when friends come over to the exclusion of almost everything else; or if you are anxious that your ten-year-old son has morphed into a lout, aping the manners of macho street culture when hanging around with his friends, don't be. It won't last! This phase is generally temporary, and the child you thought you had will reappear after a while.

Boys: Brazen and Bumptious

Once boys have grown out of the early on-off phase of friendship that affects them as much as girls, they usually have more emotionally stable and straightforward friendships than girls. Boys tend to demand less intimacy and therefore get let down less; and if they are let down they'll try desperately hard not to show it! Their nearest and dearest are "mates" rather than soul mates, compatriots rather than co-conspirators. Boys are more outwardly directed, and most would prefer to feel important through having a reputation among their peer group than be important to someone through having a close, intimate relationship. They're also more likely to be show-offs because the fame this gives them is a form of power. As they are beginning to flex their male leadership muscles, many relish notoriety, positive or negative. If they cannot make their mark legitimately, some will make it illegitimately through daring and disruption. Ten-year-olds, for example, are famed for acting up in class or playing the class clown, largely to impress and attract a personal following. Other typical tactics include challenging authority and parading over-the-top macho behavior in public places, such as spitting or swaggering around in whatever "gear" currently expresses male assertion. Bluster and bravado are the tools of boisterous boys, and they love to make others laugh and get up to mischief—most of it harmless. Boys can also be highly competitive in very overt ways. Even good friends will vie with each other to compete for a place in the team or to get good grades.

Feeling Bigger and Stronger in Groups

Boys are also a bit like pack animals; they feel bigger and stronger when they roam as a single group, and when young, many love nothing more than to have a play-fight. Some strive to become pack leaders whereas others are happy to (and are sometimes made to) follow along and take orders. These youngsters are often pleased just to be included and belong—at least until either they muster the confidence to challenge the leaders or, perhaps, they spot someone younger or a new boy keen to join whom they can push around. It is very common for the leaders to use a smaller guy to act as their messenger or undertake dirty tricks on their behalf on another group. Boys who become leaders demand loyalty and receive it as a sign of their power. It is the root of gang culture for older boys. But loyalty is also a positive aspect of boys' camaraderie: Boys can be immensely loyal to an individual friend, or to a group or territorial gang because it represents where they belong. For most boys, loyalty means keeping things they know about a friend very private and not inquiring too closely either. "Telling on someone" is certainly the worst offense, even if that person might benefit from receiving help.

Girls: *Generous (Mostly) and Gregarious, Yet Vulnerable*

If you have a daughter, you may notice that she tends to talk—*a lot*. Girls typically see themselves as groupies and form intimate, smaller-scale cliques rather than gangs. Having a close relationship, often as many as possible, is important and taken as a sign that they are accepted and acceptable. They usually care deeply whether they are "in" or "out" and whether they have a best friend; most are at their happiest hanging around with others, usually preferring company to isolation. Girls can be wonderful friends—very caring, considerate, generous, and understanding, offering real emotional support when a friend is unhappy. In fact, from about the age of ten, girls will see it as a sign of loyalty to speak to an adult to get help if she considers her friend is having trouble and could benefit from outside intervention—for instance, if they are worried about a friend not eating properly and becoming calorie and weight obsessed.

Gossip and Rumor Mongers

But there is a harsher flipside to girls' general warmth and caring: They can be prone to abuse the trust they're given. Perhaps you've watched this play out with a daughter who has had the misfortune of being on the receiving end of such mistrust. Girls can become terrible gossips as they try to gain friends, and the more they judge themselves in comparison with others, the more they're likely to keep an ear open for stories that they can use to make themselves look better. This same sensitivity to how their looks and successes compare to those of others, or the desire to be a better friend to a particular girl than someone else, will also make some younger girls gullible and easy to manipulate, too quick to believe the made-up stories that are floated their way in the form of malicious rumors. Selin, age eleven, said, "Girls have big secrets from each other. We make big fusses." Leanne offered this advice on friendship to someone younger: "If someone comes up and says that a friend of theirs has said something nasty, don't believe it straightaway. That person may be jealous of that girl and wanting to break up the friendship. You must sort it out right away." Jodie, also age eleven, showed similar cynicism and caution about what some girls will say about others. She demonstrated that the intrigue can become unbelievably contorted. "We argue over loads of things. If one friend goes to your closest friend and says you've been nasty about her behind her back, she'll think they're an angel for telling her. She won't believe you, after, that it was a lie and made up." You will find more written on mean girls and gossip in Chapter 6.

Threesomes

Friends in threes are a particular feature of girls' social lives from the age of six or so. A minefield, they can cause no end of problems. Petra, mother of six-year-old Alexandra, said, "Up to [age] four, it was okay to have two or three girls home to play, but now Alex is six I avoid three girls together like the plague. They always gang up. One always gets treated more harshly by the other two. The girls can be so bitchy, even though they're so young!" Girls (for it is usually girls who form threesomes, as boys tend to prefer larger groups) argue over a range of issues, from who likes whom best or what to play, to, later, liking the same boy. Nine-year-old Lucy said, "It's really hard having three of us together. . . . There's always someone in the middle. If the other two have had a fight, each one wants you to take sides. They then say, 'If you don't I won't be your best friend anymore.'"

Closer to adolescence, their relationships can become more intensely possessive, aping the boyfriend-girlfriend

⣿ TIPS . . . for what you can say and do

- Explain why threesomes are troublesome for everyone, even adults. If she's like my daughter, she'll be hugely relieved when you tell her that threesomes are notoriously difficult and that frequent fights are common.
- Say that the constant ups and downs and fights could make her feel inadequate and at fault, but reassure her that it's not her fault at all and it doesn't mean she has something wrong with her: It's a feature of threesomes.
- Try to make it very clear that tensions are unavoidable when three people try to be best and equal friends and would like to but cannot do everything together. It's easy to feel jealous; however there are usually simple, practical reasons why things happened in a particular way—nothing to do with one of the trio being sidelined.
- Let her know you realize it's a bumpy ride, as understanding this will help her to ride the bumps.

demands that will soon emerge. It is not surprising that threesomes can create jealousies and tensions, for it is almost like sharing one's romantic partner with another. Intimacy, loyalty, dependency, affirmation, couple identity, and even power are all evident in these tiffs.

What Girls Say About Boys and Boys Say About Girls

Boys and girls tend to be equally dismissive of each other from around age nine. Each sees their own gender as vastly superior. Girls generally look down on boys as being immature, rowdy, full of themselves, and interested only in sports and fighting. Seven-year-old Kelly said, "Girls like playing dramatic play and the boys like rough stuff." Boys sneer at girls for being wimps and goody-goodies and for spending hours wasting time doing nothing but gossiping. The boys I talked to recoiled almost physically as they described girls' "bossiness" (shades of the maternal authority that they're struggling to free themselves from) and were very vocal about the backstabbing they see flying around. Significantly, though, individual boys tended to be more tolerant and open about their appreciation of girls' different strengths—their ability to listen and understand—when discussing the differences alone with an adult. Without an audience of same-aged boys, they can reflect in a more measured way, and will admit they occasionally play with a handpicked individual from the other camp.

Boys on Girls:

Lewis, age nine: Girls in the playground are really selfish and self-absorbed. They play all the time with one person. They have big arguments and then the next day they are best friends again. One day they're best friends, next day worst enemies! They're backstabbers—talk lots behind their backs. They use their bodies and faces to be nasty. Girls give each other dirty looks and pouty kisses which say, "I don't like you." Actually, girls are mostly okay! I'm mostly closest to them.

Theo, age nine: Girls always spread the rumors around. When I look at the girls they're always lovey-dovey—arm in arm. It seems a bit different from us! You know, people think boys are rough and girls are cute, but it's not true. Sometimes girls are quite naughty: They bring big earrings into school, come in with painted nails and jewelry, and they ping their hair bands across the room. You want niceness from a friend, and they're not very nice.

Reno, age nine: Girls show off a lot. They have so many problems. Some girls took my friend away from me. They said to him, "Why would you walk with him?" and he went off me. Girls fight with words.

Cy, age ten: Girls start most of the fights and arguments here. They push. [In contrast,] we punch so we can't do it back to them!

Sean, age nine: Girls always hang around as a group. If one girl goes somewhere else, they all follow. Two best friends can fight over the same boys. Sometimes it's okay for boys to play with girls. If he does, we don't judge him or anything.

Jamie, age nine: We like to play army games and football. . . . We pretend to have guns and run away from each other in two teams. We play with girls for . . . hide-and-seek and connection. We do play with one girl—with a tomboy. She's a girl but doesn't like girlie stuff—like, she hates pink and makeup. We like to talk about football.

Dean, age nine: Girls cheat more than boys, but we still like them! Boys always hang around in a group and talk about sports in the playground when we arrive. When girls and boys fight all the time with each other, boys are always more noisy, so it's the boys that are always told off and the girls get away with it.

Aron, age ten: Three words that describe girls? I'd just say, "Very, very bossy."

Girls on Boys:

Selin, age eleven: Boys' friendships are more normal. They're kinder than we are, but I wouldn't like to be a boy!

Megan, age nine: Boys are silly and show off all the time, which gets them into big trouble. They have to sound big to impress the girls and the other boys. They don't work as hard as us.

Lucy, age ten: All boys want to do is fight and kick balls. Their brains must be empty. Don't they care about hurting people?

Aminta, age eight: Boys are so noisy . . . not all of them, but most. They love being dirty and making rude noises, and they don't seem to care about feelings.

Abigail, age eleven: Boys fight a lot. They just do wrestling and stuff. They play lots of sports and stupid things like that. They're not really like friends because they don't actually talk to each other. They just fight! Boys are horrible when they have arguments. They shout, swear, and fight, but they make up within ten minutes.

Emma, age eleven: They don't really help each other through bad times. They just let their friends get on with it if they're stuck on work. . . . They think it's cool. I think they work better on their homework than their classwork, which they rush and don't put much care into. Abigail's right about making up quickly. Girls take longer, a few days sometimes. Overnight's long enough for our school, except when it's a really big fallout.

The Importance of
Play in Friendship Patterns

Boys' and girls' friendship styles and patterns are substantially influenced by what each likes to do and play. This is inevitable because play is their prime learning and social activity. There are other influences, too, of course; for example, how each child thinks, what they find interesting and important, how emotionally sensitive they are, and how they prefer to communicate—through intimate conversation or through creating a noise and physical exertion. Nevertheless, play is what makes a child's life fulfilling, fun, and formative.

How Play Changes as Children Grow

- Until the age of about three, children tend to play alone or in parallel; they are very self-focused and are not ready to make collaborative, reciprocal friendships, though they can feel affectionate toward and comfortable with another child.
- From about age three, once they are capable of sharing play objects and expressing and sharing ideas, friendship based on mutuality can take shape. Young children will play in small groups because larger ones are intimidating.
- As they grow older and feel stronger, the group size also tends to expand. Boys' baseball or soccer, for instance, will change from a casual playtime knockabout

to being based on organized teams. Larger groups, in any case, are more complicated to manage in terms of agreeing and "policing" rules, so this type of play will not emerge until their brains can create and plan such structured ideas, which will usually be from about age eight or nine.

- Younger children's group play will be physical and/or fairly random and chaotic—for example, playing tag or kickball or acting out stories based on TV characters or on familiar family roles. There are no rules for what happens: Children bounce ideas off each other and the storyline emerges, perhaps led by the most assertive or "bossy" person in the group, which is why there can be total confusion how the game is supposed to be played.

How Young Girls Play (Ages Five to Nine)

When young boys and girls play together, girls will generally act out the female parts and boys the male ones. Sometimes they'll change over. "Family" play is likely to involve just two or three individuals, and usually girls. The game is more likely to be Moms and Babies, or Sisters, rather than Moms and Dads, so there's less chance for boys to be involved. Casey, age six, said, "We play puppy games. We're dogs and we run away. I don't care whether I play with girls or boys."

Lucy, age nine, lets off steam in the playground with her friends by playing ponies. They use jackets or cardigans looped around one or the other as reins and gallop, pony and rider, one behind the other. They also play demanding and skillful jump-rope games. These, again, are small-group or paired games focused on topics and activities typically associated with girls.

Older Girls' Play: Talk and More Talk (Ages Ten to Twelve)

Eleven-year-old Emma said that at school she and all her friends talk. That's all they do. For some ten- and eleven-year-old girls, the word *playground* is a misnomer. The recreation area should be called "the talking shop" instead! Emma reported that when she goes to friends' homes, "We sometimes cook. Quite often we play on the Play Station, actors' games. . . . We can make the characters actually move on the screen, like using a camera. Sometimes we take our bikes to the park, or we watch TV—and of course we talk, too. We often play computer games." But the computer games that most ten- to twelve-year-old girls will choose to play are very different from those that boys enjoy. Similar skills may be involved, but the storylines and the amount of physicality depicted will be very different. Eleven-year-old Katherine, for example, loves to sing along to *High School Musical* Wii whereas her brother Mikey, age nine, will play *Star Wars Lego* Wii. At school during recess, Katherine reported less interest in talking and more in being active. "We play tag. There's usually eight girls. We all play at recess. It's fun to play 'cuz we have these bases and it's fun because we test ourselves to see if we can run to the other base without getting tagged. I love being 'it.'" Another popular computer game played by girls is *The Sims,* which is based on a fictional family and allows the player to rearrange the house and create different storylines around each of the main characters. Katherine explained that at home with friends, as well as sometimes singing and dancing, "We really like to play with my American Girl dolls. We always play with my cat. We like to play outside on my swing set, and sometimes we play Frisbee. We always like to watch a movie, and sometimes we go to the movies."

How Young Boys Play (Ages Five to Nine)

Younger boys' pretend play can be very active, to the point where we get tired just watching them! Don't be surprised if your six- or seven-year-old is fascinated, in particular, by military-type games, unless of course your family prohibits them. In time, obsessions with military, animals, and so forth get replaced by more regulated and rule-governed games such as baseball, basketball, and flag football, although these often are, admittedly, organized by a school's playground assistants. Nine-year-old Mikey shared, "We play soccer. Four of us"; but when friends come to visit at home they can settle down and "like to build Legos" as well as play "sports, kickball, tag, run around outside, and eat candy!" Boys seem to have an endless supply of energy and need to be energetic most of the time. And when you are rushing about, you have little chance to do that thing you're least good at—talking—so it's a great avoidance activity on top. Of course, when the bell sounds and classes resume, they'll be fired and hyped up on adrenalin, hardly the best state of mind and body to concentrate and sit still, which is harder for them at the best of times. One mom recalled that when her son was four, she'd bought him a play kitchen. He used it, she said, not to play at cooking but to crawl into its spaces and take it apart, including removing the cupboard doors from their hinges! When the kitchen was brought out from storage to be used a few years later by his younger sisters, they played with it in the traditional way—pretending to cook and wash dishes.

Older Boys: Ball Sports and Computers

Aron, age ten, explained why soccer is so important to him. He, like many other ten-year-old boys, is obsessed with the sport:

> Watching a game is so tense and exciting. It changes; you don't know what's going to happen next. Playing soccer is very competitive, which is good. It builds your stamina. You can do lots of cool stuff with a small, round ball—flick it up onto your head, bicycle kicks. . . . It's important to be good at sports. You have to run and work hard and prove your strength by stopping people [from getting] the ball off you. . . . If you can run fast, you can get away or stop someone. It's a priority of your life to be strong so you can protect yourself. You can win awards, and the feeling when you win something is triumph, pride. It's good once in a while to feel really proud of yourself.

Playing with a ball clearly suits typical boyish boys: It satisfies their compulsion to be fidgety and enables them to focus inward on the ball rather than outward when they'd need to "read" the people and social groupings around them and chat. Even at home while playing on his own, Aron admits he'll get out his sports cards and his marble collection and create a game using one individual card character to propel the marble to another.

It is clear from Aron's account that boys in general invest a huge amount in physical prowess and sporting skill because this is an obvious way to feel male and have status within the peer group. Those who don't like sports, or whose bodies are simply not built for powerful and coordinated physical exertion, can not only feel left out but also be sidelined. These boys will feel less rejected and depressed if they achieve some success in another way. Some will develop their talent for making people laugh. Some will throw themselves into another activity, such as music, art, or computing and information technology and work to excel in that.

Nonathletic boys

It's great if your son is into sports, but if he's not, or if he's just not very good at it, he could feel very left out.

Children have to be encouraged to accept their differences and be proud of the talents they have, not to dwell on their limitations in areas that are not their forte. The more you worry about any unfair treatment they receive as a result of physical clumsiness (or even tease them at home for it), the less they will be able to gain a positive self-image.

Strong self-esteem depends on accurate self-knowledge, not pretense or cover-up.

> My child had been part of a large group of friends but in third grade was effectively dropped by the alpha males—he stopped being invited to play and stopped being invited to parties, etc. He refused to take part in the after-school soccer club, which virtually all the boys did, because he said he was no good at it—not helped by the fact that captains chose teams and he faced the ritual humiliation of always being picked last! I nearly went to the school to complain about the team-picking but someone told me that this is what always happens in the clubs, and if he didn't like it he didn't have to attend. This whole episode almost certainly upset me far more than him. I think it's very common for parents to project their own worries on to their child.—Eleanor

Alternatives to Sports

During the preteen and early teenage years, many boys become interested in the music scene, and you may find a drum set, keyboard, or electric guitar on your son's birthday list. It can be a good alternative to the sports world. Still others will intentionally or accidentally find a sport that requires a different set of skills and a context that is less physically challenging or intimidating for those who are a bit timid. For instance, David Bedford, the former ten thousand meters world record holder, took up running after being forced to run cross-country as a punishment for continuously forgetting his soccer uniform. He quickly discovered that though slim and, he'll admit, verging on the puny, he had natural stamina and a good stride that he was happy to take advantage of.

In today's world, computers and online games are popular with just about every boy from around the age of eight. The characters they can become enable them to feel powerful, take them to new worlds (ones in which adults don't interfere), and allow them to take significant risks in the safety of fantasy. The Internet and video games are now very much part of growing up. Boys can either get together to play in one or another friend's house or can meet online to share a game. Once their boys are actively engaged in cyberspace, parents should be aware that they might decide to explore boundaries and take risks in the digital world. The potential dangers of playing on the Internet and linking up with virtual friends online are discussed in Chapter 6.

Friendship Quality

Despite having differing styles of play and therefore friendship, friends are equally important to both sexes for delivering affirmation and identity and safety. Girls generally make a bigger fuss about their friendships and are more worried about whether they're in or out of favor, but boys love and need their friends just as much and value similar qualities—reliability, trust, loyalty, and kindness. It does not follow that boys' looser style of play leads to looser bonds. "My friends are what keeps me happy," said Mital, age ten. "I'd go crazy stuck indoors with my mom, grandma, and sisters." All friends represent freedom and especially, as children get older, freedom from the family. For boys, friends provide the opportunity to escape from an often female-dominated home—and the bossiness that Aron, cited earlier, associated so strongly with girls.

When a Child Doesn't Conform to His or Her Gender Stereotype

If your child's behavior doesn't seem to fit a gender mold, don't worry. Molds are created only to produce clones of an idealized type and shape, not real people. Any distress you feel about unexpected behavior could be your problem, not your child's. Your child could simply be behaving in ways that tally with a part of her that is dominant at the time, which will be helping her to feel comfortable. And while still a work in progress, a child will continue to display contradictions, queries, and quirks. This is normal. Children will frequently wish to explore different aspects of personality or preference through different types of friends, either of the same gender or by picking and mixing. Their assertive bit may mean they enjoy spending time with one type of person; their creative and imaginative side will lead them to select a second friendship that satisfies that interest, and so forth. Our children are complex creatures who face a long journey of exploration and development. Until they settle into a stable, mature personality (to the extent that any of us does!), they can remain very vulnerable to throwaway comments and criticism from people whose opinion they value.

It is important, therefore, that you show you accept your child for who he is, what he needs, and what he wants to do at that time, so avoid trying to direct his activities, interests, and friendships to "normalize" him and fit your expectations. Treating any child as malleable and available for you to fashion is exerting too much control and could undermine his self-confidence and self-belief.

Ten-year-old Carly, the youngest of three children, was in fifth grade and the epitome of a tomboy. She refused to wear a skirt and was happiest in the baggiest and sloppiest tracksuit she could find. She was tall for her age and certainly not sylphlike. She chose to have her hair cropped, as close to a boy's cut as she dared. Her size and strength meant she was at least an equal match for the boys in her year at school, many of whom were still slight and awaiting their preteen growth spurt. Carly was great at soccer and played only with boys before school, at recess, and after school. She identified with them very closely and tried to be their friend beyond the playground, though she was less successful at this. She loved to climb trees and take physical risks. For a time, then, she was without good friends at school, straddled between the girls and the boys, not quite belonging to either. Her mother was unconcerned with this situation and was happy to allow Carly to express herself freely, to find her own way. She was therefore incensed when Carly's class teacher suggested she should discourage her daughter's masculine ways and style because it might hinder her settling into middle school. In fact, Carly settled in well. When she decided she was ready, Carly naturally varied her wardrobe, comfortably befriended her female classmates, and at the same time was able to apply her obvious physical talents across a wider range of sports.

Carly's mother was appreciative of her daughter's individual ways and tolerant of these, but children's peers are often not as tolerant. Peers tend to embrace socially expected behaviors because it's easier to follow the crowd than to decide how to be different. A child who doesn't conform may be singled out. Mickie, for example, at age six, mentioned to his schoolmates he was friends with the girl who lived next door to him. Among his particular classmates, as punishment for his unconventional preference which they considered very *strange*, Mickie was cold-shouldered for two months—an uncomfortably long time for someone so young. It has to be said that both behaviors were normal. It is very normal for a six-year-old boy still to enjoy playing with a girl whom he knows well and is readily available because she lives close by. It is also typical behavior, unfortunately for Mickie, for his classmates to react with collective feigned horror.

Thankfully, in many areas and schools there is more tolerance. Lucy and Freddie's experiences show that girls and boys may still occasionally play with children from the other side of the gender divide. Lucy, age nine, said, "I have a friend who's a boy. He's Mister Brainy. He's not like the other boys, not showy-offy. Other boys think, 'You're a girl—why should I play with you?' He sees me as a friend, not a girl friend. He does play some fighting games, but he doesn't like hurting people like the other boys." One ten-year-old boy said that he'd play with girls in his neighborhood, but only those who liked to play sports. His brother, two years older, said he was happy to join in mixed ball games after school, including tennis, but school was boys-only territory. At home, with the kids they've often known for years, the social rules are more flexible.

Very occasionally, strong and repeated cross-gender attractions that persist when children typically split into same-gender camps may suggest that a child feels uncomfortable either in her stereotyped gender role or in having the gender she was born with. These will be extremely complex feelings for a child to have. Whatever explanation lies behind a particular child's friendship patterns at any point in time, and however temporary or permanent the behavior turns out to be, the only appropriate response as a caring parent is to accept your child's inclinations because these are part of your child. To deny these traits might encourage him or her to rebel or withdraw and lead to personality-linked friendship problems that are the subject of the next chapter.

5

RECOGNIZING PROBLEMS— AND WHAT TO DO

In this chapter we look at the impact of a child's, or a friend's, particular personality on a friendship. As children grow older, especially from age eight, when they tend to ignore parental guidance and choose their own friends, personal friendship patterns—how they manage friendships, the types of children they choose as friends, and what they do together—begin to emerge. These patterns may give cause for concern.

Many parents' concerns relate to passing phases and are unlikely to lead to serious long-term difficulties; however, very occasionally a parent's anxieties are justified. The first part of this chapter outlines common anxieties parents have about their children, which may lead to long-term friendship difficulties if allowed to continue, and gives suggestions on what parents can do. The second part provides general advice to parents on dealing with problems.

Excessive Shyness

Shy, Miserable, and Lonely—Or Quiet and Happy to Be Alone?

Children who find themselves on their own at lunch break with no friend to play with can be painfully shy, lonely, and miserable; be quiet and content; or simply be playing safe and watching until they've sized up the noisy, unfamiliar world of the playground before they enter it. But not everybody who stands apart is happy to be a bystander. One mother said of her five-year-old daughter when she started school, "She's a very shy person. She hated it. She cried all the time." Tammy, also five, said, "I sat under a tree and cried where no one could see me."

In surveys, children say the best part of school is making, meeting, and playing with friends: Friendships can be the feature that makes school bearable, with playtimes being the high spot of the day. For those who don't have friends yet want them, or are sometimes ignored and left out, playtime can become "pain time." If your child hates being alone, he will need your understanding and support to ensure that it's a temporary difficulty and doesn't turn him against school and studies in the longer term.

Understanding Shyness

Shy is a term used to describe a variety of feelings and behaviors—children are shy in different ways and for different reasons. Children can be born with a tendency to be more or less sensitive, but they are not born shy. They become shy because they:

- decide they don't like to be watched
- feel anxious in new situations and new places, especially when apart from their main caregiver
- feel small inside
- feel lost in large groups
- are worried about an aspect of how they look or of making a fool of themselves
- have a tendency to clam up or "lose their tongue" and are embarrassed by that

These tendencies, some of them linked, will mean that a child manages some types of encounters better than others. Peter, now eleven, remembered how he suffered when he was six. "My shyness was a lot to do with the atmosphere around me. I didn't like strange new places. I always suffer when I go to a new place, like a new school. It helps if you know someone there, but I'm always shy with the teachers. . . . In my first school it had to do with there being many more girls in the class. Girls are very different, and I felt very unsettled around them. That made meeting other children outside school hard too."

Do's and Don'ts of What to Say

Try to avoid using the word *shy:* If you tell your child he is shy, or describe him as shy to others within his earshot, he

TIPS . . . to help your shy child make friends more comfortably

- Take your child with you when you socialize—in cafés, parks, or houses—so he gradually feels more comfortable in new environments. Take something for him to do so he doesn't cling to you. But don't push him away, either.
- Keep your home life as regular and familiar as possible to help him feel safe and secure somewhere.
- Encourage him to join a small local group that offers movement, drama, or singing activities for children. This may help him to feel more confident about expressing or being himself when he's with other people.
- If you can, invite friends with children to your home, but keep the numbers low so your child isn't overwhelmed.
- If your child is switching schools, whether it is from preschool to kindergarten, elementary to junior/middle, or junior/middle to high school, try to find out in advance who else is going. Help him to meet some of these other students before they all start.
- Once at the new school, talk to the class teacher(s). The school is likely to have policies to help shy children form friendships.
- If you have time, attend any school events so you meet other parents; then if your child is invited to play, you can go too and help him feel safe.
- When a quiet child opens up and wants to talk or asks a question, give him your full attention—stop what you are doing, listen, and ask follow-up questions to explore his thinking further. If he feels he is important to you, he'll feel more confident in the company of children.
- Don't shame or berate your child if she makes a mistake.
- Try not to comment negatively about any physical aspect of your child, even in jest. Careless comments on hair, ears, or body shape can start a fixation and feeling of shame.

- Always show trust and put him in charge where appropriate. Suggest how he may develop his confidence but let him decide when to try it out.
- Find a book aimed at someone your child's age that raises similar difficulties with making friends and feelings of social anxiety.
- An older child may find it easier to develop a school-based friendship online, after school.
- Getting close to a pet can gradually help a shy child feel comfortable with other children.
- Having a friend who is younger may feel less threatening or daunting.

may not only become more anxious and thence shy but also be more inclined to give in to his fears rather than challenge them because you already see him as shy.

Avoid posing a daily question about how recess was and whether he found someone to play with as this suggests you see his solitariness as a major problem. Berating him with phrases such as, "If you weren't so shy you'd be able to manage this perfectly well" is another unhelpful approach.

To stay positive you can say:

- "Even children who seem happy can feel nervous. Everyone is finding their way. The beginning's always worst. It's not about you."
- "It often takes time to find a friend. You'll probably find one when you're least expecting it!"

- "You're a lovely person with a lovely personality. When you're ready to show what you've got inside to share with others they'll love to be your friend. You should allow yourself to feel more confident because it will be fine."
- "It's a funny thing, but one friend leads to another, so the hardest step is the first one."
- Subtly offer conversation leads—"Do you think Chloe had a good holiday? You might ask her when you see her."
- Always focus on the practical issue, not on shyness: Whether it is performing in the class play or going to a party at a strange house, find specific things to say to your children that they will find reassuring. If you talk merely about being shy, they won't see any practical ways to shift it.

Overcoming Shyness or Hiding It?

If your child once struggled with the pain of shyness and hated being alone but is now less bothered and more self-sufficient, that's great. But be careful. Children can adapt to their shyness and hide it in self-protective, but not necessarily healthy, ways. Children can, for instance, disappear upstairs when visitors arrive, claiming urgent homework, or retreat to computers or books even when a friend has come over to play.

Some people thrive on pushing themselves, forever putting themselves to the test in demanding and risky situations, but it's more common to stay within a comfort zone—a comfortable way of behaving that enables them to extend the boundaries steadily at a time and a pace that feels right. Some individuals are more wary and seem to retreat. Instead of creating a flexible comfort zone that allows gradual progress, they withdraw behind a defensive safety barrier that impedes normal development. A cordoned off safety zone enables them to avoid things they find difficult. A child who has erected a tactical safety barrier may have become a:

Clam—very quiet and withdrawn, hardly speaking and hardly present, hiding in a bedroom, head in a book or computer.
Clone—the perfect version of what's expected, won't put a foot wrong.
Clown—disruptive, to divert attention and to take control of any potentially scary situation.

If you believe your child is spending increasing amounts of time on his own, is unusually quiet, or appears to be socially isolated, with no counterbalance of healthy socializing at school, do check your concerns with the teacher. Being alone can become a habit that, over the long term, can encourage exaggerated fears and fantasies, and enable mental health problems to take hold. However, rest assured that many children feel shy. As your child's experience widens and he becomes more comfortable and flexible socially, it is very likely that his fears and yours will fade and then be forgotten.

Unbalanced Friendships

Clear-minded and Assertive—Or Bossy, Manipulative, and a Bully?

It can be hard to judge the overall feel of a child's relationship, largely because you're not always there to see it. You may be left wondering whether your child, or your child's friend, is simply assertive, confident, a good arguer, and used to getting his own way, or if he is manipulative and controlling of others, causing distress with behavior that borders on bullying.

Jostling for position and experimentation with power is, of course, an inevitable part of children's friendships. It is how they learn to hold their own and to judge when they go too far and should rein in. No relationship between human beings is ever completely equal or balanced: Even with adult couples one will tend to be stronger, sometimes in every domain and sometimes in selected areas only; and the balance of power may change radically over time. We cannot expect, therefore, that each one of our child's friendships will be perfectly balanced. Children who have several friends will find that each relationship possesses a different quality and while they may be dominant in one friendship, they may be dominated in another.

How can parents know whether a power imbalance they witness is part of the normal rough and tumble or is symptomatic of something more worrying? Psychologists have identified features that are associated with normal and healthy friendships and ones that typically accompany unhealthy friendship.

A healthy friendship exists when:

- the children show respect for each other
- there is give and take
- they can look forward to having fun, most of the time
- there is no obvious exploitation
- each child has the chance to develop in an age-appropriate, well-rounded way

An unhealthy friendship exists when:

- the same person gets her way all the time
- it imposes restrictions—"No, you can't do this" and "No, we won't play that"
- it imposes inappropriate conditions and tests, such as, "If you don't play this / go and tell that person that, I won't come to your house next time you ask me"
- one child is on constant alert for the other's short temper, mood, or emotional rejection

What You Can Do If You Are Concerned

If you are concerned that your child is in an unbalanced relationship, it is a good idea to speak to the class teacher. Chances are she may know what is going on and whether she considers it to be a problem. One teacher, Tracy, said, "I have a friendship pair in my class. One always bosses the other, and it's not healthy. I'm trying to split them up by giving them different partners for classwork. One of the moms is worried

about it, too, and came in to see me. It's better for both children if they mix a bit more." Check with the teacher about
what you might usefully say to your child at home, if anything.

If Your Child Seems Very Dominant

To help determine if there is a real problem, ask yourself
some questions:

- Does your child always like to have the upper hand,
  whether he's with his siblings, home friends, or school
  friends, in the park and when playing at home? Or is
  it just with one particular friend?
- Has his friendship behavior changed only recently? If
  so, could another child be influencing him, has he
  reached a stage when it is typical to want to exert
  power, or has something happened at home?
- Is his behavior evident in face-to-face situations only, or
  does it include telephone conversations and Internet
  contacts too? Try to look at any networking site chat
  room your child takes part in (if you can make sense of
  the odd names and words used!) to help you answer this.
- Might something be happening at home to explain
  your child's increasing assertiveness at this time?

If your child seeks to always be dominant, he may have a
problem. Ask him to consider how his friends might hear
and react to what he says. Encourage him to share at home
and play games that involve taking turns. If he's not partic-

ularly sensitive and doesn't readily "hear" or "read" other children's cues, he may need your help to recognize these and learn how to tone down his bossy ways.

If Your Child Is Constantly Being Dominated

- Invite different children over to play.
- If your child is invited to the "bossy" friend's house, find an excuse for her not to go.
- Encourage a sensitive child who is naturally kind and polite and who may hate offending anyone to speak up to protect her interests.
- Encourage her to decide more things at home, develop her ideas in discussions, and speak up for herself more confidently.

Manipulation and Bullying

A child who tries to gain advantage over another—to get his way, to feel powerful and in command, or to impress others—is manipulating them, and this can be very unpleasant.

Nine-year-old Petra described what happened to her:

> When a friend's being nasty to you sometimes and at other times being nice, it gives you a really bad sinking feeling. I'd lie awake at night thinking about it. At the beginning I'd want to start the day early, meeting the girl who could turn nasty and trying to make her happy so she'd be nice to

me. I used to make up loads of things about my family—
silly stories that weren't true—because that used to make
her laugh, which made me feel good and hopeful that she'd
be nice that day.

▓ TIPS . . . for dealing with a manipulating friend ·····

Your child will need help, but try not to dive in and take over.
Give her some things to say and do, then leave her to use
them.

- Try to be understanding. Say, "I know this is a difficult
  time." If you had a similar experience, tell her about it to
  show you can share this fully.
- Suggest that she repeats a simple phrase to herself that
  makes her feel stronger and good about herself, such as, "I
  am a kind, lovely person. She's the one with the problems!"
- Make sure your child has a happy time at home with reliable friends and family so she doesn't feel socially isolated.

Sometimes manipulative behavior can develop into bullying. Bullying is usually understood to be deliberate and
sustained negative or aggressive behavior by one or more
people who intend to frighten or hurt their victim. It always
involves an imbalance of power, for the bully controls the
victim by exploiting a weakness or drawing attention to a
physical feature that is different—hair, skin color, body
shape, a disability, or wearing glasses, for example. Bullying
can be verbal and emotional as well as physical. It is the unrelenting and calculated nature of the hurtful and aggressive behavior that defines it as bullying. A bully is openly

hostile and dismissive toward the victim and conveys hatred of the victim. Serious bullying, therefore, is rarely done by someone generally considered a friend. Eleven-year-old Peter explained:

> One boy in my class was bullied every day. He was just annoying, used to ask annoying questions. The strong guys in the class started it, one in particular who's very big headed. They took every opportunity to say something nasty, all the time. Some boys live for bullying. They believe they have the power to turn everyone else on someone else. They do it to gain respect so no one dares to oppose them. Basically, bullying is about what others think of you.

Is Your Child Being Manipulated/Bullied?

It can be hard to sort out behavior that is part of normal childhood experience and that which is exceptional. Children who have been angered or upset by something someone has said or done commonly describe the incident as bullying. This is understandable, for children feel things intensely, particularly when their friendships and standing among their peers are involved. But just because a child says he has been bullied does not necessarily mean he has. One teacher said, "A parent will often call up to say, 'My child's been bullied. She came home crying. Something's going on.' Then when I talk to the child I find it's not really bullying but instead someone saying, 'I won't be your friend anymore!'"

Rather than get bogged down in accounts of who said what to whom and how often to determine if there has been manipulation or bullying, it's a good tactic simply to respond to your child's obvious upset that you know is real. The problem is often short-lived: As children develop, they go through stages of being nastier and nicer.

What You Can Do to Help

It is very hard to know what is the best action to take. It is important to take account of both *the incident*—its severity, context, any background and persistence, and *the child*—his personality, the degree of distress, his age, and so on. It is also important to realize there is a difference between *providing support* and *getting directly involved* or engaged as a protagonist.

Getting directly engaged includes actions such as:

- approaching the school
- finding and speaking to the other child
- challenging the parents of the child

Being supportive includes:

- finding quiet time to listen
- discussing alternative strategies
- offering advice
- keeping them happy at other times to boost their confidence

Cathy, mother of then nine-year-old Rosanna, talks about her daughter being bullied:

When Steve and I found out that our daughter Rosanna was being bullied by her friend, Tessa, it was a shock and the most difficult thing Steve and I have had to deal with. We didn't know it was happening. We only found out about it after about a year, because it was only then that the school called us in, having tried to sort it out within school but they hadn't managed it. Rosanna had chosen not to tell us anything was wrong, and we hadn't spotted the signs of trouble.

We should have noticed the signs. It came to a head when she didn't want to go to school. It started with her being sick one recess. She was sent home that afternoon but didn't want to go back the next day, which was a complete change for her. We knew there'd been a bit of teasing, but we didn't think it was to do with that because we didn't know how bad it was. After that, she'd only go to school if I took her to the door and handed her over to the teacher.

She obviously couldn't manage it on her own, so we had to be understanding and help her. We talked to Rosanna, gave her some ideas of what she might say and do in different situations, yet tried to keep ourselves separate. We knew we shouldn't dive in and take over. I said to her, "I think it's a very difficult time, being nine, and I wouldn't like to be back there. When I was nine, a girl called Sharon was horrid to me." We suggested she say a few mantras to herself over and over . . . "Rosanna, you are a lovely girl" and "It isn't me who's the problem, it's them." We also made sure Rosanna had a happy time at home, and chose more reliable friends to have 'round to the house so she didn't feel totally isolated. She's more wary of people now, less trusting, perhaps, but she's come through it herself and is stronger.

Rosanna, now ten, spoke of the support she received from her parents:

Parents have to help you. I got to the point of realizing "anything's better than this," so you have to sort it out. Mom and Dad made me picture a scene and helped me to plan lines I could say. I needed courage and a bit of a push, to work on talking back. They'd suggest I say to myself: "You're not a bad person. You can do it." Once it was cracked I felt more confident. I'd built a wall in my head. I couldn't do anything when Tessa said horrid stuff to me. I was good at avoiding her but not facing her. I'd then imagine ways to outsmart her with things: "Why are you even saying this to me—because you were the one who was told off." Dad said tell her what you want to do, such as, "I'm sorry, I'm playing with this person today" and don't wait for her to tell you what she wants you to do.

My mom and dad told me what they did with their problems. They took the solutions they use, put them into my situation, then encouraged me to make them into my solutions.

Neediness and Clinginess

Clingy, Needy, and Possessive— or Loving and Loyal?

Miriam, mother of four grown children, recalled:

> One of my sons only ever had one friend at a time. He was never a team player. He was lucky, though, because when one friend had to leave the area or he had to change school, he found another individual very quickly to replace the other. He always was, and still is, the internal, sensitive one of my four children. He's in his twenties now and married, so he has no problems with relationships. They're very close and keep to themselves. You could say he's found another single friend! That's his pattern. My other son is quite the opposite—he has kept up with all his friends from elementary school onwards and always has people around him!

This boy preferred a quieter, one-on-one, deeper and loyal friendship. He didn't opt out, put up barriers, and become withdrawn or isolated. This friendship pattern suited his sensitive temperament and in no way hampered his personal development. His relationships were well balanced with no hint of manipulation.

However, children who have only one friend can be needy and possessive. Katerine, mother of six-year-old Sally, has watched her daughter try to negotiate a less easygoing friendship that contains difficult demands and pressures.

I've noticed there are a few little girls in the class who seem to stick to only one friend. Sally, my six-year-old, is in a sort of clique with five or six others and has one other very good friend too, Holly, who's also six. But Holly doesn't have other friends and won't do anything without Sally. She won't go to the ballet class or a party, things like that. Recently Holly said she wouldn't let her mom go out to celebrate a special birthday unless Sally came over to stay the night for company, so Sally felt she had to go when she didn't really want to. Her mother isn't worried at all and isn't pushing Holly to make more friends. In fact, she tries to get Holly to do all the things Sally does. If Sally gets invited to someone's house to play, I don't mention it now, because once before when I did she called up the mom to get Holly invited too. It's a bit much. My daughter is Holly's security blanket, and Holly is a bit like that for her mom, who does anything and everything for her.

A child may choose or need to cling to a particular friend for different reasons:

- A child with only one friend will be left alone when that friend plays with someone else. This won't feel nice, and to prevent that from happening, that child may demand more from the friend and cling to her.
- A child will sometimes be clingy with her peers if she has had frequent trouble making and keeping friends. She will be so keen to keep each latest "catch" that

she will try to become too intimate too soon and want constant proof of the friendship.

How to Recognize a Needy Child

A needy child may touch her friend more often than is normal, stand closer than most people find comfortable, bring in personal possessions to school to give away to curry favor, want to sit next to the friend all the time to prove the friendship and show it off to others, and interpret each kind gesture as a sign of total commitment. It can be exactly this cloying style that puts other children off and may cause yet another budding friendship to fail.

Teachers are aware of clingy friendships and consider them generally unhelpful because they may restrict other friendships and prevent a child from becoming either stronger through learning to rely less on just one person for safety or wiser by experiencing a variety of friends. Mandy, currently teaching six-year-olds, said, "There are two kids in my class I think are too clingy. I called in the moms about it. Children need more variety at this age. They're a bit too exclusive."

Teachers have experience but are not always right; they may not be aware of the subtleties of different personalities. Nonetheless, if your child has plenty of opportunity to forge wider friendships yet still seems more comfortable attaching closely to just one friend, accept this as his personal pattern.

▦ TIPS . . . to help a child become less clingy ············

- Try to make important family relationships as regular and reliable as possible.
- Explain that good friendship doesn't have to be proved all the time. A smile can be enough to show interest and affection, and if a friend talks to another child it does not mean he has been forgotten.
- Tell him frequently the aspects of him that you find so lovable and how important he is to you. If he feels loveable he will have less need to curry favor and "buy" friendship through inappropriate giving.
- Demonstrate through small gestures that you think about him while you are away from him—that you keep him in your mind. "While I was at work this morning, I remembered that funny thing you said that made me laugh so much last night. It made me smile again!" This will help him to feel more secure with his friends while they are not in his physical presence.
- Don't encourage your child to curry favor with friends by letting them do risky things at your house.
- If you believe your child is being seriously hampered by clingy habits and is often tearful over failed friendships, consider speaking to a relevant professional about the situation.

Antisocial Behavior

Normal Mischief or Serious Misbehaving?

Children have an unrelenting fascination with the forbidden. Young children especially love to explore things that are declared out of bounds and to experiment with getting close to banned objects or places, such as electrical sockets, low cupboards, or steep stairs. Exploring danger is also part of having fun, learning common sense, and experiencing self-regulated control—they have to learn to judge things and stop themselves rather than simply respond to a parent's command. If your older child is using his increasing strength and confidence to master the things that used to frighten him, exploring the possibilities of his newfound independence, even to see what he can get away with, it doesn't mean you have a delinquent in the making. It is absolutely natural for children to test the boundaries, take measured risks, and flirt with danger, especially when they are with friends and old enough to have more independence. This is very different from knowingly defying the law and intentionally threatening their own or other people's safety.

Actions we might put in the "mischievous" category can include such things as:

- knocking on doors and running away
- straying beyond agreed upon play areas
- throwing small sticks at dogs or cats
- strewing toilet paper around someone's front yard
- putting something slimy into a parent's bed

Just because these forays into the forbidden could be passing does not mean you should turn a blind eye, however: Pointing out the potential dangers and problems shows that you have noticed their behavior, consider it foolish and dangerous, and that it's not okay. Then let it rest more or less at that to show you trust them and expect them not to go that far again.

Signs of Deeper Trouble

Signs that your child could be getting into deeper water with potentially deviant friends rather than paddling at the edge with mischievous and curious ones include the following:

- getting into fights and other trouble at school
- standard of schoolwork low or falling
- being angry and hostile toward you and/or the teacher
- avoiding school
- occasionally playing truant
- lying and stealing more than occasionally, and stealing from you
- smoking cigarettes
- drinking alcohol
- teasing and harming animals
- spending a lot of time out of the home, wandering in the park or streets
- playing by roads, rail tracks, or rivers doing daredevil tricks
- seeming unusually interested in matches and fires

The ideal action will depend on the age of your child. It is easier to direct a friendship when children are younger because you control their time more closely and they're also more amenable. Older children may not be so compliant.

■■■ **TIPS . . . for if your child regularly chooses**
■■■ **rebellious companions**

Whatever the age of your child:

- Give your child a more positive sense of self.
- Show her more acceptable ways to have fun.
- Encourage alternative friendships without overtly criticizing her friends.
- Make your own values and rules clear.

Having more independence, they may ignore a command that forbids contact and end up listening to their friend more and you even less. Instead, use more subtle tactics, either to break the pattern of the relationship or to address and replace the pleasure your child gets from belonging to that group and behaving in that way.

Stay Well Clear or Get Involved: General Advice on What to Do If You're Worried

Stay Tuned to Your Child

Listen to Your Child

Children's views matter, because it is their life and difficulty. Six-year-old Adam said, "If someone hits me and really hurts me, I tell my mom and she says don't be his friend. But that's unfair because Darian and Kit can be really nice people, very nice friends, too. They can be aggressive—but nice, too. They just sometimes hurt people who annoy them." Suki,

∷∷ Additional tips for dealing with older children ········

- Arrange other activities—for instance, get them to join a club or arrange family outings—at times when the friends usually meet.
- Discuss the nature of friendship and why some kids like to pressure others to join them in doing wrong.
- Ask why they enjoy the time they spend with this particular gang of kids and what they gain from the friendship.
- Try hard to improve your child's self-image if that is negative. This could be a possible cause for teaming up with certain friends.
- Try to spend more time with them on their own doing fun things, especially activities that they're good at, to emphasize that you enjoy their company and appreciate their skills.
- If you are a single mother and worried about your son's behavior, try to find a suitable adult male role model—a relative, friend, teacher, or neighbor—who can give him some personal attention and show an alternative way forward.

age five, also mentioned fairness: "Diana, she can be a little rough. My mom likes her mom, but she tells me to stay away from her. It's unfair, because I do like her a little bit. But I always do what mom says." Twelve-year-old Alice provided the view of someone older: "Parents shouldn't try too much to get involved, unless it's something serious like physical abuse, because it is important that you learn to deal with these kinds of people, and parents can make things worse." Katherine, eleven, said, "If I see one of my friends get bullied, I go right over and say, 'You think you're so cool but you're just hurting their feelings.' But sometimes my friends can stick up for themselves. I'd want to get my parents in-volved if somebody every day was stealing my lunch and I talk to my teacher and it keeps continuing."

Watch for Tell-tale Signs of Difficulty

If a child is very upset over a friendship problem, she won't be able to hide it. It will slip out in changed behavior, even if she tries to keep it to herself. As a rule of thumb, up to about seven years of age, children will be open and likely to tell. From then on, they are more likely to be wary of telling. Older children often believe they should be able to manage these things, which not only increases their embarrassment of failing but also adds a shame element because they take it more personally. Given that they are now more aware of adult problems, older children may try to keep something to themselves to avoid burdening a troubled parent further. Keri said, "My dad always told me that I should feel able to talk to him at any time about my problems. I nearly told him about them in third grade, but it helped knowing I could tell him when I decided to. I don't know why I didn't." In fact, her father had recently experienced some business problems and her mother was pregnant with a third child. Either of these situations could have explained her reticence.

What to Look For in Younger Children
- becoming more anxious or clingy
- crying more
- changes in eating or sleeping patterns

- strange pains in odd places, legs or hands, as well as head and tummy
- wanting to get away from school quickly at pick-up time

What to Look For in Older Children
- wanting to be taken to school instead of walking there
- finding excuses for staying at home, especially on a Monday
- talking themselves down—about looks or schoolwork
- feeling or being sick
- worrying about how they look and wanting to lose weight
- a sudden drop in school marks and attention to homework
- having disturbed nights
- bed-wetting, nail-biting, renewed thumb- or finger-sucking
- losing school equipment frequently, because it's being taken
- wanting to take things into school to give away

Don't Jump in Straight Away

The best default advice is not to jump in straightaway. Instead, show that you understand your child's unhappiness or difficulty and keep note of what you are told and see. In general, parents tend to worry too much rather than not enough, which is entirely healthy and not at all surprising, because your instinct will be to stand up for your child and protect him or her.

However, if you become too closely involved you could end up with:

- An embarrassed child. Exposing his difficulties could be a message to classmates that your child is not coping, which could backfire and make matters a lot worse. This happened to someone in Peter's class. "One classmate, who was generally annoying, had his ruler stolen. His mother stormed into the classroom the next morning waving a receipt for a new one! My friend whispered to me, 'What a wimp.'"

- A child who clams up and tells you nothing ever again. If you get it wrong, you might never be entirely forgiven. You might also lose the friendship of any other parent involved. Sandy, for example, e-mailed a mother to advise her of her son's insistent bullying behavior and suggested she do something about it. "She made such a fuss and went to the head teacher saying I had no business to contact her. It's taken me eighteen months to get to talk to her again, and we're still not friends." Sandy's son said, "Boys don't tell parents anything. They don't trust what they'll do. Anyway, boys like to play tough—to pretend that everything's fine."

- A lost learning opportunity for your child that can boost his confidence. He won't discover his ability to solve his own problems, or discover that difficulties often fade with time and are more easily endured with that knowledge. With the benefit of hindsight, most parents will admit they were overly concerned. For example, Ruth said, after her son was teased for a while for being overweight, "Actually, I really felt this was quite a useful episode in retrospect because you've got to be able to cope with teasing and that's not going to come naturally to everyone."

You can usually gauge the seriousness of a problem by whether the school calls you in. If the teachers have spotted a problem and they believe they need to discuss it with you, they consider it serious. However, quite often, and more so as a child reaches the age of nine or ten, a school will try to solve a friendship issue as an internal matter without involving you, especially if a teacher senses that's what your child would prefer. As friendship spats are often temporary and relatively trivial, the school may not want to bother you. Rest assured that you will be called in if the problem persists. Of course, if your child is unhappy or struggling at any time and the teacher hasn't noticed, it would be sensible to mention it discreetly so you can have an on-the-spot pair of eyes checking the seriousness of the upset.

Sound Principles of Involvement

Remember that involvement is not the same as engagement. Support and understanding are forms of involvement and are good responses. Direct engagement is rarely advisable.

1. Don't fight your child's battles for her. Unless your child is being seriously threatened, your job is to listen and empathize and offer things to say and do, but not to fix the problem. Generally, these ups and downs are part of the growing process.

2. Don't criticize her friends, however awful you think they are being. When you criticize a friend, your child hears you criticizing him for his choice of friends, which is liable to make him defensive and uncertain. Acknowledge that the friend can be nice and hurtful.

3. Look for distress but don't judge the size of the problem by its momentary intensity. Children don't have the same sense of proportion as adults and can't fine-control their emotional responses either. The tap is either full on or full off. Time is usually a better judge and measure of seriousness than most children and even many parents!

4. Assure him that what's happening and what he's feeling are normal, without belittling his distress, so he doesn't feel the odd one out.

5. Empathize. Show you understand how he's feeling by saying something like, "I'm not surprised this has made you feel . . ."

6. Shore up your child's self-esteem. Make a special effort to praise and appreciate strengths and talents and offer plenty of love, time and affection.

6

FRIENDSHIP AND
SOCIAL PRESSURE

The previous chapter looked at the impact on friendship of a child's or their friend's particular personality and how parents can sometimes worry about what this may indicate for the future. Here we consider a selection of practical dilemmas that parents face daily as children encounter today's social and commercial pressures and other families' approaches to life. It ends with a section on the social pressures that parents face.

Social Pressures on
Children's Friendships

The scary part for parents as our children grow older is watching our control gradually slip away. Having decided everything from what our daughter wears, what and when she eats, to what she plays and who with, we watch as the power shifts inexorably to friends and peers. As well as becoming her own person, a child starts to *prove* that she's capable of being different from us—which, of course, she is—even to the point of open conflict: From around the age of eight, she'll often prefer to fight her parents than be different from her friends. Peers become paramount because children want to fit in.

Peer Pressure

Good friends will think similarly and like the same things and may therefore be very happy to "do their own thing" together against the crowd; nevertheless, it's unlikely they'll be completely immune to trends. Social antennae, sensitized to what others say or do, never entirely switch off. If others are seduced by the next must-have item, they could be, too. If your child's friend becomes more status conscious and susceptible to trends—and has parents who generally give in when pestered—your child could be cast aside if you don't allow her to follow suit. Until a child becomes more certain of who she is or how to act, the prevailing social pressures are particularly strong. As Molly, now eleven, remembered about being eight, "At that age you're very, very sensitive," which also explains why spiteful comments can cut deep and why, more than anything, most children's worst fear is being different and being picked on for that reason.

What You Can Say to Manage Peer Pressure

- "I understand that you want to be liked, but it's not healthy to give in or make yourself uncomfortable in the process."

- "If she's a genuine friend, why do you feel you need to pretend? If you start being this way with that person, and that way with this person, you could lose track of what makes you 'you.'"
- If the things she wants you to do pile up, offer choices: "I'll say yes to the thing that matters to you most, but that's all. What will that be?"
- Suggest he says to a pushy friend, "My mom or dad won't let me." Many children prefer to be protected from pressures and "looked after." Don't be scared to be firm.

When They Want Something a Friend Has That You Don't Want Them to Have

Although most parents enjoy pleasing their children, constantly giving in to children is not helpful to them in either the short or long term.

Typical battles can concern matters such as wanting the latest fad, wanting to dress in mini-sized teen fashions that are now marketed at younger children, or wanting to watch movies on DVDs or play computer games graded way above their chronological age—because "everyone else" is allowed to see or play them. Eleven- and twelve-year-olds may want pierced ears or bellies, or crave the latest model cell phone, TV, or computer game, despite the current model owned working satisfactorily. Children's birthday celebrations can be another area of competition and pressure.

Other Families' Views and Values

One mother complained recently, "The hardest part is not, actually, being pestered to buy a particular item my ten-year-old wants desperately to have because it's the current fad; it's having my values challenged. My daughter now sees that there's another world out there—that other people and other families do things differently—and she prefers their way because she thinks there's more in it for her. It's really hard to stick to my principles in the face of the pressure. I don't always agree with what other parents are prepared to allow."

What You Can Say and Do

It may seem strange to state it, but when handled sensitively the battle that follows a denial can strengthen your child's sense of well-being. However angry your child may feel at the moment of refusal, deep down he will prefer to feel looked after and know he's part of a caring family that has clear beliefs and practices. Parents who dither and then give in may not provide that healthy sense of security. Growing children also need to experience disappointment and see they can live happily without that "must-have" or "must-do" thing. This can strengthen their self-esteem, whereas giving in can feed anxiety. Just as important, children who cannot cope with disappointment make life more difficult for their friends, who may then decide this friend is too much like hard work—and move on. If children learn to define success and happiness by what they own or by a passing pleasure, their happiness won't last. They may be angry, but it will usually pass: They don't hold grudges against a parent or caregiver for long, and most parent-child relationships are not destroyed by one dispute, certainly not at this age.

If you want to turn down a request for something, couch your argument in terms of beliefs and values rather than discipline and disapproval. If you sound punitive or ridicule her wishes, she could feel put down and might turn against you through more general defiance. Better to say something like:

- "I really don't think having this is the right thing for you just now. I know you're worried you'll be left out and you want this really badly, but your friends will soon be onto something else and they'll forget."
- "A good friend will let you be different and still like you. Do you feel ready to try this out?" She may answer no but consider your suggestion afterward.
- "Every family's different, and we're like this. We prefer to wait for birthdays and then give things you really want as a present (or let you stay up later, etc.). I believe in our way. It wouldn't be right for us to change just because you feel pressured by friends. Just tell them your mom or dad won't let you. Most kids accept that."
- Don't criticize the friend or the friend's parents personally. Focus any concerns on precise actions, choices and disagreements, not on prejudice or personal styles.

- Avoid trampling on their sensitivities or scolding them for wanting to be like their friends. "I don't care what your friends—or you—think. This is how it's going to be!" is not the best reaction.

You can also explain the power of advertising and marketing, and that companies pay child psychologists to tell them how to make children want things. They also use children to start fads and trends among their friends and now use social networking sites to pitch specifically to children. Marketing is a very powerful tool. If an issue is really important to you, stand firm. However, it certainly shouldn't always be "no." Often, merely stating your arguments and concerns can be enough to show them where you stand: "I've told you what I think and believe. You can see I'm not happy with this—but it does seem particularly important to you, so I'll agree." School fads can be useful in helping your child make friendships when she might be struggling. I have a friend whose child was very bright, not athletic, and generally thought of as a bit strange. She resisted all school trends on the grounds that they were a waste of money, but she did give in on Pokémon cards—and her son forged friendships with boys who'd previously ignored him. Some of these friendships lasted way beyond the Pokémon fad.

If the desired item soon falls out of favor, point out the lesson that's there to be learned. Be aware that the next friend will probably like something different, or that the same friends will soon decide something else is a better thing to have or do, costing less or being more age-appropriate.

A good, longer-term protective strategy is to nurture our child's personal values and sense of self so he is better able to identify and resist inappropriate pressures when they arise. The healthiest response is to set out the issues, explain our view, invite our child to present his own view, and then to stay true to himself as he weighs the options and we review ours.

The Pressure to Impress

Children can feel even happier—for a moment, at least—if they set a trend or ratchet it up a notch. A young child may peddle exaggerated stories of what his family owns, what they've done together, or even who belongs to his family, creating a fictitious relative, sibling, or parent. An eight- or nine-year-old is more inclined to angle for a special birthday party, an exotic family holiday, or a bigger and better sleepover. And older tweens are prone to tell fibs about what they have done to sound more daring and mature. If we sense our child is becoming competitive in this way, reassure him that he is great as he is and needs no extra trappings. If you give in, you could deepen, not dispel, insecurity because it suggests you agree that these superficial things matter.

Birthday Parties

These days, the annual birthday party looms as a major life event for five- to seven-year-olds and beyond. In an age when other parents hire magicians, traveling petting zoos, and moonwalks, the pressure to have your child's party live up to the last birthday party he attended can be intense. If you don't give time to think through the various issues carefully, the day can become a let-down and disaster, not a pleasure. Annie, age five, talking about her best friend, said excitedly, "It was her birthday. We went to this place and went on the big slide and it got dark and we screamed! It was very fun! I'm having my next birthday party in a museum. My last one we went to *Charlie and the Chocolate Factory* and had surprise chocolate there." Redon, age six, remembered, "My birthday was in McDonald's. I forgot to invite Luke, but I invited Callum and John, Jordon, and Joshua. My brother's eight. He had his birthday at the movies." Celebrating a birthday and being the center of attention seems particularly important when you are so little and often overwhelmed by living in a big person's world.

Among the danger points that arise over birthday parties are these: Who decides who comes (should your friend's child come even if the birthday child doesn't like her)? Who decides how many to invite and who's left out— should you invite the whole class to avoid upset? Should it be a sports activity, or will those who hate sports feel left out? Should family finances be stretched to allow a hired venue for a party, or should a home-based party, if there's room, be made acceptable? What can you say if your child feels let down by the kind of event you feel is appropriate and within your budget because he wanted something more elaborate to keep up? And there are other children's parties to manage, too, especially when one invitation is accepted before another arrives that your child would prefer to go to. Do you let him pull out?

Remember that this party is for your child and is his event, not yours—even though you are hosting it. Once children are old enough to complain about any of your suggestions as to who should come, the guest list should be their choice and should comprise their friends, not reflect your guilty conscience. At the very least, the names and numbers need to be raised, explained, and discussed. Inviting the whole class to avoid upsetting any child could be taking tact too far, for a party of this size is usually impractical. And at some point, children need to be comfortable with the reality that they won't be asked to every celebration going. Similarly, we should not feel the need to shield a child from the economic realities of life. The birthday boy or girl should have the chance to appreciate that it's possible to have fun creating a theme-based party at home instead of spending more on a fancy activity-based occasion or entertainer. To help make the event seem theirs, children might help to design the invitations, either on the computer or on a sheet of paper that can then be copied. Ten- and eleven-year-olds are often capable of organizing their own party, planning the games and food.

Peter, age eleven, said, "I've only ever just invited a few friends to my birthday party, about five or six people. I've always done that. I think you can have more fun . . . with a smaller number." Smaller parties seem to work best for young children despite parents occasionally wanting to show that they can organize larger parties. Young children can be overwhelmed by too many guests and too much going on—and thereby become the forgotten star as the often complex organization takes first place.

Sleepovers

From about nine years of age, and especially among girls, sleepovers sometimes become a badge of status and sophistication. A sleepover is a cross between a party and a play date—a sort of nighttime (and often nightmarish!) pajama party. The prospect of hosting or attending one fills kids with wicked anticipation and an intense excitement as they fully expect the usual rules about bedtimes and behavior to be waived. That's exactly why parents typically hate them. Sleepovers become the measure of true friendship in middle childhood not only because of the close physical contact but also due to the necessarily limited number that can participate and therefore the exclusive, private nature of the fun experienced.

Although it's natural to be slightly uncomfortable about sleepovers, they can be very beneficial. They give your child a valuable opportunity to spend the night away from his parents in a safe environment. Often at the end of elementary school or the beginning of middle school, children will be given the chance to go on a school trip and spend a few nights away. Schools do this to encourage friendships, to help children bond with a new school, or as a fun treat in reward for all the hard work put in during elementary school. Having managed such a trip, I know that children seem more confident and mature afterward. If your child is too anxious to go, he'll miss out. Sleepovers will give him a chance to get used to being away from you.

⠿ TIPS . . . for coping with sleepovers

To minimize the potential hassle factor of sleepovers, consider these tried and tested tips:

- Sleepovers symbolize growing up, but eight-year-olds can still get very homesick. To avoid returning the unhappy ones who can't stay the course at some ungodly hour, or pulling another parent from bed, start with a friend who lives close by. Make sure his favorite cuddly toy is also invited, and any other comforter or familiar pillow.
- Reserve sleepovers for Friday nights or school holidays, as children who stay up late are likely to be exhausted the next day and unable to cope with very much.
- If your child claims he wants to go but then his confidence collapses, let him pull out. Sleepovers are passing pleasures, and children will learn they can remain friends without joining in everything. There will be another occasion.
- If the sleepover is at your home, state clearly in advance what the ground rules will be about lights out, midnight feasts, talking after dark, and morning antics.
- Have the guests' parents come to collect them the next morning as early as possible at an agreed time—though they'll probably want to make the most of their sleeping in! You don't want to become a free next-day babysitter as well.

DVDs and Computer Games

If your child pesters you to watch a movie certified as suitable for older children to impress their friends and feel cool, hold firm. It is valuable to wait until close to the advised age in order to retain some personal authority and to demonstrate respect for public guidance and the law. Always check with other parents if their child is to watch a video or DVD recommended for older children at your house.

Gossip and Rumor Mongering

Hannah had been lively and happy at school with plenty of friends, but at the age of nine things went horribly wrong. A lonely classmate who was jealous of Hannah's popularity started a series of false rumors at her expense to take over her friends one by one and leave her isolated. Jenna would take someone's work, sports kit, or pencil case and then claim that Hannah had stolen it. With another, she falsely confided that Hannah had been two-faced about her behind her back. Hannah was neither slim nor fashion conscious, which Jenna quickly exploited to label her as a "loser." Hannah began to be excluded from parties and sleepovers, and finally she was deserted by every friend. Jenna was remarkably successful. Hannah's parents eventually realized that she needed a clean sweep and moved her to another school, where she resettled well and made reliable, new friends.

Gossip mongering and spreading malicious rumors are typical tactics used by children in middle childhood to feel on top, especially among girls. Children can be mean and are sometimes tempted to take out their personal problems on others. Becoming the class gossip puts them center stage: in-the-know and therefore able to impress others. They often target those with natural self-confidence whom they are jealous of. But even those whose lives seem favored can exploit someone's weakness when they feel the need to get an edge. Girls also indulge in social gossip, which is rather different—a common and usually harmless way to network and exchange information between friends.

How Children Harass

Knowledge is power, and older children can use "facts"—real or made up—to increase their status. Sensitive personal information, such as a parent losing a job or a sibling being in trouble, can be ruthlessly exposed and exploited. Nine-to twelve-year-olds can fabricate malicious falsehoods about their target, usually in an effort to suggest the person cannot be trusted to be a true and reliable friend. Another common tactic is exaggeration. For example, by spreading the story of a hyped-up version of a class member's exotic holiday that ridicules the envied experience, the targeted individual will be deflated and left feeling foolish rather than fortunate.

Girls are more prone to use gossip and rumor for personal benefit as they are generally more natural schemers, more likely to abuse trust, and more prone to self-doubt. Boys tend to seek status through physical or sporting prowess and notoriety, so their tall stories—usually about sporting achievements or daring—generally flatter themselves rather than undermine others. They can, though, target and tease classmates who possess a gentler disposition as "gay" while they struggle with their own concerns about their male identity. Unfortunately, as girls and boys get older even the time outside of school provides little respite. Cell phones, text messages, and instant messaging make it easy to twist the knife 24/7, as we see below.

Help your child to be true to herself and to understand why the harassment may be happening. Once she has a clear sense of her own values and feels good about these, she will be able to stand her ground with more confidence. Explain, too, that some children at this age and stage may need to target others or might have a personal problem that inclines them to dominate. It certainly helped one nine-year-old girl I interviewed to believe that a classmate had been unkind to her because that child's grandma had Alzheimer's disease and no longer recognized her. The victim, who loved her grandmother deeply, imagined this would feel awful.

If you learn that your child is being mean, provide plenty of appropriate attention. An unconfident child often finds it harder to mix comfortably so ends up lonely and possibly more likely to spread mean rumors.

Cyber Foes: Online Stranger Danger and Bullying

A key feature of communicating via the Internet is that it allows people to disguise themselves and either be anonymous or masquerade as someone entirely different, which raises immediate dangers for children being targeted by

::: TIPS . . . for if your child becomes the butt of gossip and rumor

- *Take your child's feelings seriously.* Insults and untruths can hurt deeply. Assure your child that it is the instigator who has the problem and that she is not to blame.
- *Shore up your child's self-esteem.* Understand that your child might be moody as she copes, and try not to add to her burden by being critical of her behavior. Instead, compliment her strengths and talents.
- *Respond simply and consistently.* When teasing or gossip highlights your child's lack of some "must-have" or "must-do" thing, give one simple, supportive reason for why she can't have or do it, and stick to it. Further reasons weaken the others and can create confusion.
- *Listen, empathize, and offer suggestions* of possible tactics and things to say, but don't "fix" the problem.
- *Monitor offensive messages.* If your child receives mean-spirited text messages or chat-room gossip, remove your child's phone for a while or stay close when she's online. If messages contain threats, save or print these out and report the harassment to your child's teacher.
- Should you decide to approach a parent directly, both you and your child should agree that's what your child is comfortable with.
- Agree to an assertive phrase to use, such as, "Yes, this *is* happening to me / my family, and it's teaching me stuff, like how to stand up to the real losers around here!"
- If she feels down or betrayed, *focus on the positive.* Together write down her strong points and successes and the names of friends who are or have been loyal and kind.

classroom bullies, rumor mongers, or predatory pedophiles. Many schools now run programs on safe and appropriate use of the Internet.

TIPS . . . for how to protect your child from online bullies and predators

- Avoid having a computer in your child's bedroom—it is far too private. Keep it in a communal area.
- Don't allow children in elementary or middle school to have a webcam, which could be used inappropriately.
- Let your child know that you are interested in what they do and play at the computer and may therefore come and look at any time.
- Encourage them to tell you if they're concerned about anything they encounter online.
- Your daily interest and involvement in your child's life is the best protection against a stranger trying to exploit any loneliness or resentment by seeking trust, claiming interest, and offering a close relationship.

What you can say to your child

- If you are messaging and a stranger or someone who describes themselves as a "friend of a friend" asks to be let in, *just say no.*
- Keep personal details that you put on your site to an absolute minimum—no cell phone numbers, no reference to your school's name.
- You may not recognize or understand which conversations are suggestive. Ask for a view if you are not sure.

- Never arrange to meet anyone in real life whom you have known only online. In a recent survey, 12 percent of 11–16-year-olds said they had met up with someone they had met in a chat room or on a networking site.

Social Pressure on Parents

Though most parents will experience many of the pressures their child struggles with, because they're on the receiving end of demands and distress, they also have their own set of pressures to contend with. For instance, parents can become almost as competitive over birthday parties as children and can feel great pressure to spend as much on a particular child's party present as their parent spent on your child's present. Then there's the pressure to reciprocate—to have a child over to play because your child went there, even if he doesn't want to return the favor. It can also be difficult to deal cleanly with the problem of your child not liking your good friend's child and not wanting to visit them, with or without you. In embarrassing and difficult moments, try to remember that your first responsibility is to your child, not to other mothers or to your friends, and you need to demonstrate that you respect his views. This doesn't mean you have to bend to his will on each occasion, but you must listen to him, acknowledge his "take" on the other child, give him a satisfactory answer if you want to reject his refusal, and be fair. Social niceties can be important, and if you want him to go to play nonetheless, he can learn that doing something he doesn't want to do can often be less unpleasant than he anticipated.

"We have an only child living just a few doors away who often asks our child to play. We know the parents well, and really like them, but my child doesn't like their son—who my son says is very dominating, much better at football, and teases him all the time. When we do make him go, he always seems to have a good time. Should we respect our child's wishes (he doesn't like him and doesn't want to go—in which case we'd really have to tell the parents that) or carry on making him go?"

It is also important to acknowledge and maintain a clear boundary between you and your child. She doesn't have to like someone that you like, and vice versa. Your good friends should be able to see that you are not responsible for all that your child feels and does, so honesty is really the best policy and certainly preferable to conjuring up endless excuses. If you are ever tempted to rise to the bait of social pressure and become competitive, against other parents as well as assisting your child to keep face or get an edge, your child could copy you. Although competition is natural and can be healthy once self-worth is strong, if a child senses that his acceptability depends on his maintaining a front, his self-worth could be weakened.

A last word to end this chapter: Having at least one strong and healthy face-to-face friendship is the best way to protect a child against any kind of social pressure or unpleasant exploitation, whether these occur online or at school. The skills children use in forming and maintaining friendships and developing these in daily activity at home are the subjects of the next chapter.

7

ENCOURAGING FRIENDSHIP
SKILLS AT HOME

Making and keeping friends is a tough and testing business, even for adults. We need a huge amount of confidence to feel comfortable in any situation, especially a new one. We have to work out what someone might want or expect from us, spot where they're vulnerable, and know when to be honest and when to hold back to avoid upset. If we want to take a relationship further, we need to believe that if we like someone, they might like us. With longer-term friendships we can worry that our friends don't necessarily feel as strongly about us as we do about them. It takes many different senses and understandings to judge and manage ourselves in relation to others.

Children are bound to make mistakes as they learn and mature along the way. Parents can do a lot to help, both by modeling friendly ways in the home and by actively encouraging the sorts of actions and attitudes that foster healthy friendships. This chapter examines the skills and attitudes friendship entails and lists the behaviors children say make them avoid people, then discusses how the helpful qualities, skills, and traits can be encouraged at home. It concludes with a detailed look at the specific tactics needed to manage the common, separate stages any successful friendship must pass through, from the beginning, making these tactics appropriate in each case to the four age-related phases of friendship that were discussed in Chapter 1.

What Friendship Entails

Some children are able to get along with others apparently effortlessly. Others find it excruciatingly hard to approach someone or to know how to get close enough to forge a special bond. The majority of children are in between: They muddle along, sometimes having a hard time, sometimes having no issues. Even the most sociable child can find herself alone, self-doubting, and sad if her best friend is not in school for a few days or if they have a temporary falling out.

One way to identify the qualities and skills that enable children to make and maintain friends easily is to consider the characteristics that people typically associate with someone who is a good friend.

How to Recognize a Good Friend

I've compiled this list from the conversations I've had with children. A good friend:

- lets you have other friends
- will share and give things back

- doesn't get upset and difficult when they don't get their way
- thinks about you when you're not spending time together
- makes you feel liked and safe by smiling at you
- helps you to have fun—makes you laugh
- listens to your ideas and accepts them
- allows you to make a mistake
- will accept an apology and forgive you
- will make you feel better, not worse, if you do make a mistake
- knows what upsets you and is understanding
- can see things from your point of view
- won't put you down or tease you in a hurtful way
- is interested in what's good for you, not what you can give them
- won't press you to do what you really don't want to do
- lets you be alone, if that's what you feel like
- understands your limitations—how much you can do—and won't try to shame you or make you feel silly

A child doesn't have to demonstrate every single one of these attributes in order to be a friend; in fact, someone who did would be far too nice to be real! And someone who set out to fulfill each of these roles would almost certainly lose sight of himself in trying to do so, and come across as groveling and ingratiating.

The Qualities and Skills That Lead to Fun and Friends

As we have seen, the skills needed to help friendship flourish become gradually more sophisticated as children mature. Generally, children start to understand a concept at around the time they start to need it. For example, it is only when, at about eight or nine, a child begins to need security and commitment from his friends and the notion of loyalty can be understood, that a child will mention *loyalty* as something he values and will realize he might need to be loyal in return to keep his friend. A second example is tolerance of others' needs and views: Until a child stops being egocentric and can see himself as similar to but different from others (rather than assuming that everybody else is exactly like him) he won't appreciate that someone might see things differently. The previously valued qualities remain almost as a precondition of friendship, but they're added to at each stage of development. Ten-year-old Shardae said, "A friend is someone you can trust with secrets, who's kind." As we saw earlier, Ellie, eleven, said having a friend is "When you borrow things together, their personality is kindness and sharing and they listen to you."

The Blocks to Friendship

From the conversations I have had with children and professionals, children can erect barriers to friendship when they:

- say mean things
- don't share
- keep other children out of games
- avoid others if they're worried about what they'll think
- don't know how to pursue a friendship and keep trying
- are quick to lash out or lose their temper
- brag—show off and lie
- fail to spot the cues to friendship
- can't cope with setbacks and disappointment
- fear being rejected
- complain a lot and are frequently down and moody
- are overly bossy and demanding
- have poor social awareness and are too close/clingy, manipulative, and over keen to acquire a friendship

One group of eleven-year-olds I interviewed agreed about a particular girl in their class whom no one much liked. Their various comments included: "She's annoying, bossy. She keeps pinching and punching people. She makes fights for no reason and then gets you into trouble. She shows off. She tries to pretend she's rich. She's weird. She does weird stuff with her shoes and she eats her hair. She gets—forces—people to beat her up. She smiles all the time. She's always laughing [no matter] whatever's happened to her. If a teacher tells her off she just laughs. It makes them mad." This group indicated they'd given up on her, having tried to include her, but now they steer clear to avoid her strangeness and random minor assaults.

In another school, I heard similar comments from a different group of ten- and eleven-year-olds: "There's a boy who's not liked. The girls go around touching people saying they're passing on his germs. He picks his nose. He's quite a comedian so I still like him, but he goes too far. There's a boy . . . in the class and he calls him 'dog breath.' It's not nice." Considering a girl in their class, they said, "She kind of bullies. She bullies people to make people her friends. She always annoys us, steps on our feet. If she asks to play we say yes but she often spoils it. She doesn't know how to play games. We tried to be her friend and then she bullies us. She paid her brother to bully us. He walks past us and hits out at our bodies as he passes. She steals work from people's tray, because she's jealous." But one individual showed more insight and sympathy. He intervened, saying, "I think she's just reacting. She's doing the stuff which leads them to do things a certain way, then she reacts. It's a vicious circle. I think she has problems with friends because she hurt a friend quite badly by accident when she was younger."

These comments may seem a little harsh, but what I found interesting was the lack of cruelty or bitchiness in the discussions. Instead, the children were being factual and descriptive. They didn't like children who hit or bullied, who brag, or who behave strangely. Children clearly feel safer with what's normal and predictable. In both groups there were children who were prepared to show kindness and give someone another chance to play with him or her, provided the rules were respected. One or two showed a surprising insight, wanting to understand why someone might behave in that unhelpful way. This is good news: It shows that it is a child's behavior that makes him unpopular, and if he can be helped to change his ways, his classmates will quickly respond and change their views to accept him back.

Modeling and Encouraging Friendly Ways at Home

Parents and other family members can play a significant role in helping to develop the social and communication skills elementary school-aged children need in order to be friendly and "friends aware." When a small group of eleven-year-olds were asked how parents could help, Joshua replied very confidently, "Parents should raise them in a way that they could see how to get friends."

The typical family is not a permanent haven of peace, love, and light. Siblings fall out with each other—sometimes over friends—and couples inevitably argue. All this provides useful lessons. The best model a family can offer children to help them survive and thrive in friendship is not extreme politeness and endless generous gestures but honesty, respect, a forgive-and-forget attitude, paying attention and showing understanding, and using nonviolent means to sort out conflicts. "Best behavior" is what is required in unfamiliar or formal company, not among friends and family. However, that does not mean that disrespectful, bad behavior is acceptable or desirable—it is not. To achieve a happy medium, families should aim to show:

- tolerance of mood and moment

- the ability to feel regret and to forgive
- respect for personal and physical boundaries
- a willingness to sort out difficulties without using humiliation or violence

Sibling Rivalry Over Friends

It is very common for children to like other children who are older than them, and to be flattered if older children show an interest in them. If your child has a friend over and his older sibling is there, with or without a friend, you need to be sensitive to the fact that the friend and older sibling might pair up. Children therefore are inclined to guard their friends with their life when they bring them home, especially once they reach junior high. The worst humiliation would be, as eleven-year-old Chloe said, "That my friends will like my older sister more than me." Chloe was not so much concerned that her sister would try to steal her friend as by how likable she was. Worries about siblings taking friends are hardly surprising, given that friends are akin to possessions—"She's *my* friend." I even heard one jealous and resentful adult say to another, "*She was my friend first!*" When my sister moved close to one of my friends and started to spend time with her because they had sons the same age, I was quite discomforted. Try to be sensitive to this, and if one of your children has a friend over and the other doesn't, accept that there could be jealousy and fights, with one going out of his way to irritate and upset the other's good time. Try to arrange an alternative special activity for the one left alone—perhaps he could do something with you; and try, too, to ensure that the child with the friend has clear space to play without interference.

TIPS ... on house rules for friendly homes

- Practice sharing along with respect for rights, personal property, and personal space.
- Say "sorry" without too much prompting—parents as well as children.
- Include fair play as a central value.
- Compliment and appreciate children and don't put them down.
- Allow "rough and tumble" but not intimidation and bullying.
- Always get everyone to ask before they borrow anything and to make sure it is returned.
- Allow a child to say no to lending or doing something if he feels his interests are compromised. At least hear his reasons, and insist only after a fair discussion.
- Encourage siblings to say "well done" to each other when appropriate.
- Have fun when playing games together indoors and out.

Developing Specific Qualities and Traits

Encouraging Smiles

From the start you can give your baby the experiences that will help her make friends later. Children say repeatedly that smiles matter: They oil the wheels of friendship, so making your family an open and smiley one is a good start. Give your baby plenty of time with you in one-to-one, close "face play," looking into her eyes and holding her gaze, showing love and encouraging her to smile and trust your love. Once they are a few months old, most children find adults' put-on funny noises and funny faces hilarious, and they enjoy being surprised by the noises some toys make. Encourage babies to explore and have fun by touching different textures with their hands and feet. Early friendship is also expressed through feeling comfortable close to another child. When you are with friends and their children, position babies to lie or sit side by side on a rug rather than seated on your lap or strapped in a bouncy chair.

Children are likely to smile more if you often smile at them and if you encourage having fun. Some children, however, naturally have a more serious disposition and prefer to become involved an absorbing activity or conversation rather than seek out faces or make jokes. You have to accept and work with this.

Encouraging Play

Play is so important for children's healthy development that it is, in effect, children's work. It is what friendship is founded upon, because it is what children do when they get together, particularly up to the age of eight. They don't sit and discuss the weather or what they had for breakfast unless asked to— they begin chatting as they collaborate on an activity or game. When one child does something with another and they enjoy it, that person becomes an immediate friend. Remember Theo's observation: "At preschool you become best friends in five minutes." If your child has had, and continues to have, plenty of opportunity to play a range of things with you, with any brothers and sisters, and also with other children, she will be able to get over the first hurdle. She will have a comfortable way into friendship and a good understanding of what needs to happen next to develop it.

Encouraging Kindness and Caring

Younger children read a lot into smiles, but, as we have seen, they place enormous value on kindness. Children learn how to be kind in part by being treated in a kind way. When you think ahead about your child's wishes and show insight and care by meeting these, he or she will start to think about what someone else might want and feel and begin to anticipate this, which is the start of empathy. Parents and caregivers can point out acts of kindness in books or films. You can encourage your child to look after teddies, dolls, and other soft toys in pretend play and treat them well. *Do you think teddy is thirsty / hungry? Should we give him a drink from your cup / a bite of your apple, too?* The aim is not to force a child to be kind, caring, and considerate to others always, regardless of their own interests, but to have an emotional capacity for kindness and a clear idea of the actions and gestures that convey caring and kindness.

Encouraging Sharing

Why Is Sharing so Difficult?

From about age eighteen months, children will show people their toys as a way of saying, "*This is what I've got. Come and see it. Yes, you can hold it too.*" Showing is easier than sharing and comes first. "Show and Tell" sessions are part of the week in kindergarten to encourage children to be sociable and to express themselves by talking about something they really like.

Sharing is harder to do because it represents not simply giving away something he perceives is his but also losing a bit of himself, which can happen only when a child realizes he is a separate individual, at about two years. Once he can comprehend "me," his toys or food will become "mine," a personal possession that represents his separateness and is therefore something worth protecting. That's why the business of sharing is far from simple and when the trouble starts.

Children have to learn to share very different things, for instance:

- *time, space* (bedrooms) and *attention* (parental and teacher)
- *food*, especially snacks and sweets that they love
- *success*, through accepting they can both win and lose in games
- *toys* and other possessions

But even with things they own, they'll be more or less reluctant to share depending on how much they value the toy or object, perhaps because of who gave it to them (their favorite toy from their dad), what they got it for (a treat for doing well, after Mom got home from hospital), whether they had to save up for it or how new it is. If they're in the middle of playing with a particular toy, they'll be loathe to relinquish it until the play is brought to a natural end. Parents tend to want to show, even show off, their child's generosity by asking him to share something really special, but many adults keep their own most treasured books, clothes, cars, or trinkets well away from others.

Sharing as Power

Sharing sometimes turns into giving (you don't share a potato chip from a bag, you give it away—you can't both eat the same chip!), and there is a big difference between sharing a little bit, where you keep the lion's share, and dividing something in half, which symbolizes equality. So sharing can also encompass power and control rather than generosity, and pointedly *not* sharing could be a clear tactic to make someone envious. By the time a child has a well-established identity, at about age six, he should find it easier to share; however, the ten-year-olds I talked to spoke often of the importance of having things such as games, rulers, and erasers returned, using the terms *borrow* and *lend* more than *share*. Possessions matter. This isn't surprising given the complex links between sharing, power, possession, and identity.

Sharing Tests Trust and Equality

Parents may see sharing as a sign of generosity, but children can use it to negotiate their relationships: "If I share this, he will share that," or "He is nice enough to share things with me, therefore I can rely on him to be nice to me in other ways." Offering to share and seeing if it is reciprocated tests the potential balance in a relationship—and balance is important. When a child becomes desperate to acquire a friend, she's sometimes over-generous. Instead of appearing impressively kind she can frighten her target away with an unnatural generosity that can't be comfortably reciprocated.

Helping a Child to Share

The ability to share is important to successful friendship, but children shouldn't be forced into it. If a powerful adult forces a child to share, he won't learn useful lessons about personal identity and equality, and it could trigger arguments. Don't forget that sharing is difficult for all children at the start and they get better at it the more mature and secure they become. Boys may well find sharing more difficult than girls because they may be more attuned to power and are likely to protect their self-image, even at a young age. Sharing could be seen as giving too much. If you believe your child has a significant problem with sharing—not just toys but also attention, success, and space—and he doesn't seem to be growing out of it, think what might lie behind it. Try to enable your child to share in a way that preserves his comfort and self-respect. Your approach will need to be effective on two levels: strengthening his self-worth and identity, so possessions aren't of such great importance to him, and letting him see the purpose and advantage of reciprocation. Try to let your child decide when and how much he shares and with whom. Don't force anything.

▓ TIPS . . . on helping a child to share

- Time and attention: Try to preserve some one-on-one special time for each child.
- Toys and possessions: Keep it clear who owns what in the family and respect this ownership. A child who feels he has little of his own at home over which to feel pride of ownership may become more possessive of classroom toys. When friends come over, identify which toys are special and put them well away. Have out only the ones he's happy to have others play with. If he can't tell you, remove his usual favorites and tell him these are special for him. *House rule: Don't use anything that belongs to somebody else without asking.* Ensure that any older siblings respect his belongings; if they don't, he'll become more possessive.
- Treats: These are for him and his keeping. Don't demand he share these.
- Food/snacks: *House rule: Don't eat food in front of a visitor without offering to share.* If you want something now, it must be shared—otherwise wait and eat it later.

It can be especially hard for children without siblings to learn to share. They don't have to share their parent's attention with brothers or sisters, or share space or food at home. To avoid your child becoming overly possessive and selfish, one option is to ask her to give you a cookie or treat from her package. If she is reluctant and you don't want to insist, start by sharing your snacks or special treats with her. Special treats should remain entirely hers, but incidental snacks or games should, in time, be shared freely.

Encouraging Turn-taking

Turn-taking is an important friendship skill because it encourages children to:

- develop a general sense of fairness
- play fair
- stick to the rules of a game so it can continue for everyone
- think about other children's needs, not just their own
- be generous in defeat
- learn to be less egocentric and control impulsiveness

Taking turns is also more complex than first appears. Letting someone else have a turn is a form of sharing, and a child needs to be able to understand the reasons for it. Different games involve different rules about taking turns, some of which are highly elaborate and others not. Even talking and listening involve taking turns if you are not going to dominate and put people off. A young child's lack of patience and inability to cope with complex rules can trigger strong emotions—anger and envy, jealousy and disappointment. How many times have you played a game with a young child when she has run off in fury with the dice, shaker, ball, or other part of the game to sabotage it and to stop anyone else from winning?

Waiting Your Turn

Waiting in line for your turn—to get lunch, an ice cream, a ticket for a carnival ride—is the simplest form of turn-taking. Young children may find it hard to wait, but at least they see everyone else in the same boat. When families have meals together at a table and the food is served from main dishes, a child has to wait for his turn to be served; if you then ask him, along with the others, to wait until everyone is served before starting his food, that evens out the wait. When children eat separately or plates are filled first then taken to the table, there's less opportunity to teach this form of turn-taking.

Give and Take

Playing anything together involves give and take, or reciprocity. Whether the activity is doing a simple jigsaw puzzle, building things, painting and drawing, or even water play at bath time, you can show a child how to take turns: "It's my turn to use the red paint pot / crayon / water

squirter now." "Now it's your turn to add a jigsaw piece."
You can play picture dominoes by simply taking turns to lay
down matching pieces, disregarding alternative rules.

More Complex Rules and Turn-taking

A game such as Chutes and Ladders involves a number of
rules that confer both advantages and setbacks: shooting up a
ladder to gain spaces or sliding down a chute to go backward.
Some relatively straightforward "first to the finish line" board
games involve missing a turn as a penalty, meaning the oppo-
nent gets two turns in a row, which can be hard for a child to
accept at first; however, later lucky throws can show it is possible to get ahead again. For children up to the age of eight or
so, it is fairer to play games that are based on chance (random
turning of cards or throwing dice). Avoid games that involve
judgment and forward planning and tactics until a child is
older because they can be intensely frustrating and older and
cleverer minds will always win. Playing a broad range of
games within the family will help a child who hates to lose or
not get her own way to become more laid back, which in
turn will help her to maintain friendships.

Encouraging Trust and Trustworthiness

Children are wary of people they feel they can't trust,
which is hardly surprising. They want to know that their
possessions and their private information are safe, and they
hate to be let down when someone fails to fulfill a promise.

It is not difficult to help your child learn to trust others and be trustworthy. When you provide opportunities for him to do tasks and he completes them responsibly and well, he begins to see himself as capable and someone who can be trusted because you have shown that you trust him. Try to offer small responsibilities that increase as he grows older. A child who is usually trusted will also be more aware when he has not behaved in a trustworthy manner and is more likely to accept full responsibility for his behavior.

TIPS . . . that focus on trust

- Trust your child's competence—his ability to achieve something. "Shall I help you?" sounds supportive but suggests he might not cope. "Call me if you need me" is better.
- Trust his ability to complete or remember something. Even if he has not managed before, don't allude to that. Always let him start with fresh, positive expectations.
- Trust his judgment as far as seems sensible.
- Trust his sense of responsibility and ability to help, both in and outside the home, with, for example, tidying, clearing, meal preparation, and grocery shopping.
- Don't let him down. Keep to your promises and encourage any other adult who has an important relationship with your child to do the same.
- Don't tell untruths to get you out of a corner.

Encouraging Self-esteem and Confidence

Helping a child to make friends or acquire friendship skills sometimes involves working less on detailed skills and more on a child's core self-esteem and confidence. At any age, having friends is not only about how to be a friend but also about feeling happy with who you are. If you like yourself enough to feel others will like you, they probably will. Children who are self-doubting and reticent are harder work. Young children are often too busy to make an effort with someone who they feel needs encouragement to play. In any case, they would not necessarily know how to do this. Especially in the humdrum environment of the playground, they need quick solutions to their play needs, so someone who is

In the British *Child of Our Time* television series, one boy, almost eight, was very unhappy at school. He had only one friend to play with if he didn't want to be alone, and because he did not like to play sports he felt generally excluded and was sometimes picked on. His mother made a special effort to boost his confidence. She was able to change her job to spend more time with him; she complimented him frequently on his lovely personality and sense of humor; she encouraged him to play plenty of physical games out of school so he felt stronger in body as well as mind; and she signed him up for a boys' club, which enabled him to gain badges for skills in practical tasks and made him feel more competent—and he loved wearing the uniform. The boy's confidence soared. When he returned to school after the summer break he felt different: He was ready to throw himself into football and contribute freely and comfortably to the group play and banter. He became one of the boys and gained plenty of friends. His reticence had vanished and his popularity was secured, entirely through his mother working on his confidence rather than specific skills.

bouncy and fun and can be approached easily will be near the top of their list. Someone who hangs around on the outside of a group, who has a worried face, and who fears that he won't be liked or accepted is bound to have a harder time forging friendships. Such a child sends very clear signals that he's uneasy in this particular company. Children don't necessarily dislike an unconfident child. But they may sense that it's simpler and easier just to keep out of his way.

It is not very easy to pick a child up when his confidence and self-esteem are at rock bottom, though the preceding story illustrates one approach that was successful. More usually, though, a child's lapse in confidence will be temporary. There are several books that offer advice on how to raise a child's self-esteem. As a guide, focusing on the following areas will help considerably:

- Explain what's happening.
- Be an example to them.
- Praise their achievements and appreciate who they are.
- Encourage play, because through play children find out who they are, discover what they can do, and realize they can manage on their own.
- Trust them—assume they can and will, not that they can't and won't.
- Be affectionate—lots of hugs and smiles.
- Give them plenty of your time to talk, play, and just hang out.
- Compromise—don't fight and try to win every battle.
- Empathize—see things their way to show you understand.

Tactics and Skills for the
Four Stages of Friendship

Regardless of a child's particular age, the most appropriate practice and support will depend on the stage the friendship has reached. Friendship entails the following four stages:

- making the first move
- clinching a budding friendship
- keeping a friendship going
- coping with quarrels and arguments

If your child is having difficulty at one or more of these stages, different skills and tactics will be needed to help him progress. These are now explored in turn, with a child's age in mind. It may be helpful at this point to refer again to the list of friendly behaviors at the beginning of this chapter.

Making the First Move

For many children, making the first move is the hardest bit, rather like stepping onto an escalator: Once you are on it, the rest is easy but knowing how to measure that first stride to avoid falling over and getting gnarled up in the works can be scary.

Clinching the Friendship

It is one thing to approach a possible friend and be welcomed, but then both parties need to follow through so that

▦ TIPS . . . for helping your child make the first move

Ages three to six:

- Give your child a small toy to show to another child. A couple of toy cars, a small plastic figure, a soft toy, a little ball—all can get a conversation or activity going between two children who are each on their own. This is especially useful for a shy child or easily tongue-tied child.
- Suggest he approaches someone else who is also on his own. Find out if there's a buddy bench or friendship corner in the playground where single children can gather. There may be someone he likes the look of but who's usually playing with others.
- Timing is important. It is always better to ask someone to play before the stampede out to the playground and before they get involved in a game.
- If there's a group game already under way, a child can say, "That game looks good, can you show it to me?" which sounds stronger than, "Can I play, too?"

Ages six to nine:

- Encourage your child to be chatty with her study buddy in a lesson and be helpful. If they can work together, they'll be able to play together and then be friends together.
- Suggest they talk about interests. "I like doing . . . what do you like to do?" Tell your child not to give up too quickly. It might take him a few tries to show he's really keen.
- Help your child realize that the other child will probably feel as shy or uncertain as she does—and that these feelings don't necessarily indicate a lack of interest in being friends.
- Encourage your child not to be too direct or wordy: "I like you. Could we be friends?" or "That was fun—does that

(continues)

(continued)

mean we're friends?" are both less pushy than "Can I be your friend?" or "Will you be my friend?" though these might also work.

Ages nine to twelve:

The children in this age group whom I spoke with offered many suggestions for making the first move toward friendship, including these:

- "I'd choose someone who likes the same sport."
- "I'll look for someone on his own."
- "I'll go to the computing and technology or math club [or any other school-related or extracurricular club] to find someone like me there."
- "I'd go to someone and say, 'Would you like to be my friend?'"
- "I'll be friends with the brothers of my sister's friends."

the friendship turns into a longer term commitment. Here are some tactics that might help a child of any age to follow through, enabling a liking to become a friendship. Remember: It is up to your child to decide which tactics to use.

- Invite someone home to play.
- Say something nice about the person.
- Say you enjoyed playing with her.
- Be helpful.
- Be open to other people's advances and "clinchers."
- Invite her to play in the park with you, with an adult supervising.

- Ask the teacher if you can work with that person on a project.
- Invite her on a family trip.
- Have her visit for a play date and stay-over (if there's room).
- Have her come over on the weekend or on a day when there isn't school.

Care and Maintenance: Working at It

"I never realized how much it takes—the giving and taking, the pushing and pulling, the compassion and understanding—to keep a friendship going," said Jenny, age fourteen. Her father's job required the family to move often, and only when they eventually settled down did Jenny discover the need to work at maintaining a relationship. "Giving and taking" requires tolerance and flexibility, a sense of proportion, and not demanding you always get your way. "Pushing and pulling" describes the juggling for dominant position and coping with the resulting tension. "Compassion and understanding" is looking behind any difficult behavior for its possible causes, accepting someone else's point of view, and accepting people's weak points as well as strengths.

Coping with Arguments

Children fall out with their friends all the time over anything and everything. Mostly they find their own way through. Aaron, age seven, said, "You can be a good friend and then fall

TIPS . . . for helping your child maintain friendships

Ages three to six:

- Show you're sorry through smiles, going up close to your friend, putting an arm around him, or giving him something.
- Be helpful.

Ages six to nine:

- Play fair and say "sorry."
- Share well.
- Forgive mistakes.
- Tell a teacher if a friend's upset.
- Think about the friend's feelings.

Ages nine to twelve:

- Play fair and say "sorry."
- Say "well done" when a friend deserves praise.
- Be understanding and tolerant of "off days."
- Remember to return items that have been borrowed.
- Buy special friends a very small gift when away on vacation.
- Keep to commitments.
- Be sensitive to friends' individual personalities.

out. You have a couple of days not being friends, then I'll try to go up and say 'sorry.'" Casey, age five, described a complicated fallout but explained that afterward, "We gave smiles to each other and we all shaked hands." Samantha, age seven, said of her best friend, "If we argue we walk away, calm down then walk back." Jo, age nine, said about his friend, "He's not always kind. He's been rough three times. Once we wound each other up." Jason, also nine, said, "We're so close that sometimes we fight—like brothers. If we fight we know we won't split up. It's just okay the next day. We don't even say 'sorry.'"

Brandon, age six, said, "Once, Owen bit Marshall in the lunch line 'cuz Owen wanted to stand behind his friend Alfi. I didn't mind. It matters who you stand next to, and he said 'sorry.'"

Michelle and Sarah, both nine, have been friends for five years yet still argue and fall out occasionally. Michelle remembered they'd "broken up" about three times. "But we just have to be together. We don't say 'sorry' even. We just go back." Seven-year-old Sandra commented, "Friendship can never break—it has an invisible contact that's made of metal. You can't just press a button and break it."

Falling Out As They Play

As children spend most of their time together playing, it's not surprising that they often fall out over play. They can disagree over what to play, get confused over the rules that apply and do things wrong, or storm off because what one child's idea of what would fit with a pretend story another thinks spoiled it. Some children make up nasty rules as they go along to make someone look stupid. Younger children seem to accept their friends' outbursts; older children are more judgmental, less tolerant, more defensive, and sometimes over-sensitive to potential insult.

Parents often offer helpful tips to their children. A ten-year-old explained, "Once I had an argument with my friend. My mom said, 'You can be friends again if you're nice to each

"I have a best friend called Stash, and we were playing armies, but when playtime stopped we had to go indoors. Next day at playtime I ran away then I pretended I got shot and lay on the bench. Stash thought I'd run off, didn't know it was the game again. Then we made up together. He did forgive me."

—Lewis, age six

"We argue about what to play. I say 'I just won't play with you anymore,' then after dinner we say, 'Sorry, I'll play your game' and the other says, 'No, I'll play yours,' then we fight again!"
—Alannah, age seven

"You'd always be playing something their way. When my friend Jessica got angry and cried, they told her she was a baby so she'd run off, and they'd think it was hilarious. They'd plan something mean for her while they were finishing their lunch. We'd play heel races (running on your heels) and they'd say Jessica's always putting her whole foot down when she wasn't. If you do this three times you have to go back to the start. But then they'd block her so she couldn't even run."
—Emily, age nine

other. Say sorry,' which made me realize that friends are important to play with, so I sorted it the next day." He found that advice very helpful, yet it's hardly sophisticated conflict resolution! Ten-year-old David said his grandmother cheered him up after a fallout by making a funny joke.

Understanding Compromise

A compromise is sometimes seen as a "giving in" and being weak, but it is not. A child who can compromise is not a

⣿ TIPS . . . for helping with friendship fallouts ··········

Ages three to six:

- Explain how young children react instantly—they usually don't mean any harm.
- Have your child say "sorry."
- Encourage your child to give the friend some small token (nothing too elaborate!).
- Suggest that your child give a hug to the friend.

Ages six to nine:

- Compromise—my way this time, yours next.
- Forgive and forget.

Ages nine to twelve:

- Compromise—you want this, I want that. Here's where we agree . . .
- Understand, and make allowances for, the personality involved.
- Apologize if you're in the wrong.
- Have the confidence to step away if the friend's not right for you.

softie—she's mature and strong. It shows she can understand the other person's wishes, point of view and feelings, and looks for the areas of overlap but can hold onto her central interests. The result is that each side involved gets at least some of what it wants and is satisfied.

There is a danger that a child who's strong inside and doesn't need to force a win—and who's been brought up to be compliant—could give way too easily and be exploited.

In particular, the adjective *good* is often applied to girls who generally agree, who don't easily express anger and are disinclined to fight their corner. Some boys, too, can attach less importance to winning, and because they're not so bothered they concede. If you bring your children up to avoid conflict and to compromise, you must also make sure they know it is honorable and respectable to identify their core interests and argue for these in order not to lose sight of themselves.

Home, it's said, is where the heart is. It is certainly where most children develop the heart—the confidence and the inclination—to make friends, for it takes a great deal of courage and self-belief to open themselves to someone and face the risk of rejection. At home, we can also help our children to possess warm hearts, to be caring and considerate of others, to care about fair play, to help them fit in, yet be engaging personalities who are able to have fun. Giving children our time and talking to them as well as playing and reading with them; hearing and respecting their views and showing we care about what they think; sharing our favorite snacks; and trying to understand and settle their frustrations as well as to contain them—all these help our children develop the necessary attitudes, skills, and behaviors to learn yet more when they forge and develop their special friendships. Schools work hard both to promote social skills and to reduce bullying so children feel safe. The more practice we can give our children at home, the happier they are likely to be.

EPILOGUE

As a parent, I find it impossible not to be affected by the anguish that most children will suffer at the hands of friends at some point during their elementary school years. I hope, though, that this account and explanation of friendship styles, phases, and common and typical issues is sufficiently reassuring to put most of your worries to rest and that the tips will have provided you with tried and tested ways to support your child through any rough patches. As you have seen, there is much you can do behind the scenes to help smooth your child's way, although it shouldn't be forgotten that the struggles and strains of friendship are a necessary part of growing up, and that children learn and mature through these experiences. Their anguish tends to fade more quickly than you would expect; and, most important, children generally cope with the rough and tumble of their peer relationships far better than parents think they can. Knowing this, you may now find it easier to stand back and be the calmer, steady listening point for your child.

I hope, too, that this book has been fun to read. Sadly, it's rare to hear children's voices in books written for parents.

Those children who spoke to me and who appear here expressed themselves with such delightful directness and fresh enthusiasm that I still smile each time I read their statements, and I certainly learned much from them. If the book has made you think about your own present and past friendships, even better. It is a fascinating subject. Most of us have treasured and valued friends, and most of us, I suspect, would agree that these friends are crucial to our sense of fulfillment and well-being—so much so that we should have no difficulty in accepting the central status of friends in our children's lives. This should help us to realize that while one of our most important roles is to nurture our child's self-esteem and confidence, another is to encourage friendships. The two are linked, of course, because self-awareness and confidence form the bedrock on which healthy friendships are built. When our children proudly present us with their friends, we should welcome them warmly into our life: They can be great fun!

BIBLIOGRAPHY

Parents

Elman, N. M., and E. Kennedy-Moore (2003). *The Unwritten Rules of Friendship: Simple Strategies to Help Your Child Make Friends.* London: Little, Brown, and Co.

Hartley-Brewer, E. (2005). *Talking to Tweens: Getting It Right Before It Gets Rocky.* Cambridge: Da Capo Lifelong.

Rubin, K., and A. Thompson (2003). *The Friendship Factor: Helping Our Children to Navigate Their Social World—and Why It Matters for Their Success and Happiness.* London: Penguin.

Professionals

Bukowski, W., A. Newcomb, and W. Hartup (1996). *The Company They Keep: Friendship in Childhood and Adolescence.* Cambridge: Cambridge University Press.

Dunn, J. (2004). *Children's Friendships: The Beginnings of Intimacy.* Oxford: Blackwell Publishing.

Frankel, F. D., and R. J. Myatt (2002). *Children's Friendship Training.* London: Routledge.

Pahl, R. (2000). *On Friendship.* Cambridge: Polity Press.

Vernon, M. (2005). *The Philosophy of Friendship.* Basingstoke, UK: Palgrave Macmillan.

Children

Four to Eight Years

Child, Lauren (2008). *You Can Be My Friend*. New York: Grosset and Dunlap.

Krasny Brown, L., and M. Tolon Brown. *How to Be a Friend: A Guide to Making Friends and Keeping Them*. London and New York: Little, Brown, and Co.

Thomas, M. E. (2007). *The Friendship Trip*. New York: Grosset and Dunlap.

Ward, N. (2004). *The Ice Child*. London: Chrysalis Children's Books.

Nine to Twelve Years

Rushton, R. (1994). *You're My Best Friend—I Hate You*. London: Piccadilly Press.

Zimnik, R. (2007). *The Bear and the People*. New York: New York Review of Books.

ACKNOWLEDGMENTS

My biggest thanks must go to all the children and young people who were happy for me to hear their stories and experiences. Many of their names have been changed to protect their identity, but I would especially like to mention Emma and Emily, Abigail, Aron, Theo, Molly, Alice, and Peter. This book could not have taken the shape that it has without the children's collective honesty, humor, and insights, and it certainly would have been far less fun to write. Their contributions helped to correct quite a few early misconceptions, which is why it is essential to respect and listen to children at any age. I also need to thank the heads and staff of Capel Manor, Muswell Hill, and Newington Green Schools who were so welcoming and so generous with their precious time, reorganizing whole afternoons in order that I may talk to as many small groups of children of varying ages as possible. It is a continuing privilege and delight to be able to see schools in action and to talk with children in their familiar surroundings.

Various friends were willing to reflect back on the friendship issues their children had grappled with and moved on from, providing a very useful longer-term perspective. For more specialist knowledge, I was very grateful to be able to meet with Judy Dunn, a psychologist and author who has studied children's friendships, to discuss her findings and share ideas; and I benefited, too, from receiving useful research papers from Susie Weller and from Christine Doddington and Julia Flutter. Ruth Williams at Piccadilly Press was the instigator of this project, so I must thank her for widening my horizons.

As a parent, it's inevitable that I draw on personal experiences past and present. My eternal gratitude goes to my children, Stephen and Georgia, and to Julia and Katie; to all my friends and family who have helped me to treasure friendship; and especially to Richard, who tolerates and supports my preoccupations with his renowned good humor.

INDEX